THE PRIDE LIST

EDITED BY SANDIP ROY AND BISHAN SAMADDAR

The Pride List presents new works of queer literature to the world.
An eclectic collection of books of queer stories, biographies,
histories, thoughts, ideas, experiences and explorations,
the Pride List does not focus on any specific region,
nor on any specific genre, but celebrates the great diversity
of LGBTQ+ lives across countries, languages, centuries and
identities, with the conviction that queer pride comes from its
unabashed expression.

'Because "reason will only take us so far", in these sharp, witty and heart-breaking plays, Danish Sheikh immerses us in the affective lives of law—in particular, the law that criminalized homosexuality in India until 2018. Through glimpses of the many queer lives that are shaped in ways both direct and subtle by the violence of the law, Sheikh forces the law to confront the complex realities of these lives. Lurking beneath the frequently self-deprecating humour of his characters is a profound meditation on the weighty afterlives of a law that ostensibly no longer exists (or does it remain forever enshrined in some deepest recess of the psyche?). Brace yourself for a ride through contempt, pride, shame, love, repair and a range of other emotional states for which we do not yet have names.'

Rahul Rao, Reader in Political Theory, SOAS, University of London

'*Love and Reparation* offers any law teacher a rare opportunity to discuss with students the elusive relations of law and life. *Contempt*, the first play in this volume, demonstrates the necessity of drawing methods of text and performance together to illuminate how a trial is both an event of law, and also a form of political story-telling about how people's lived experiences are exposed or transformed when they come to law. In my own experience, as an audience member, and as a teacher of the text, this is a work that stages informed, critical engagement with law, and important collective conversations about personal and public responsibility.'

Ann Genovese, Associate Professor, Melbourne Law School

'Danish Sheikh's work shows that it is possible to think law, literature, and love together—and to do so with vulnerability, compassion, and intelligence. These plays bring together incredibly disparate philosophical questions, political movements, and popular culture, anchored by a commitment to justice. In the world of *Love and Reparation*, the courtroom becomes a place of more than confession and prosecution— it becomes a site of storytelling and the imagination of alternative possibilities for justice.'

Daniel Elam, Assistant Professor, Comparative Literature, University of Hong Kong

'How does law, whether it is the law contained within legal statutes, the law of love, friendship, communitas and strife, or the symbolic in psychology, insinuate itself into our queer lives, loves and longings? Using the conceit of the dialogue and the dialogic in *The Symposium*, Plato's Greek play on love, Danish Sheikh dramatizes something beautiful, tender and extraordinary in these two plays. The Platonic dialogue on love frames and orchestrates both plays—and through them the playwright makes us witness, participate in and feel the myriad stories through which queer lives shape themselves before and after the sodomy statute was read down.'

Geeta Patel, Professor, University of Virginia

DANISH SHEIKH

Love and Reparation

A THEATRICAL RESPONSE
TO THE SECTION 377 LITIGATION IN INDIA

LONDON NEW YORK CALCUTTA

Seagull Books, 2021

© Danish Sheikh, 2021

Foreword © Tarun Khaitan, 2021

First published by Seagull Books, 2021

ISBN 978 0 8574 2 750 2

British Library Cataloguing-in-Publication Data
A catalogue record for this book is available from the British Library

Typeset by Seagull Books, Calcutta, India
Printed and bound in the US by Integrated Books International

If therefore thinking it absurd
To identify
Law with some other word . . .

Like love I say.

Like love we don't know where or why,
Like love we can't compel or fly,
Like love we often weep,
Like love we seldom keep.

W. H. Auden, 'Law Like Love'

Performance of *Contempt* at Oddbird Theatre, Delhi, 3 June 2018. Photograph by Prateeq Kumar. *Reproduced with the photographer's permission.*

CONTENTS

FOREWORD

Power—whether political, social, cultural, economic, material or epistemic—can be exercised for good as well as evil. Even so, power has a propensity to aggrandize itself that predisposes it towards evil. One way to constrain power is through power itself.

Another is through law.

Law is necessarily an expression of power. But in genuinely democratic contexts, it is likely to be an expression of the power of *multiple* wielders. This feature gives it a more dynamic character. Further, law admits to a normative critique a lot more readily than power itself, even if only to enhance its perceived legitimacy.

Love and Reparation poignantly explores this duality of law— its ability, at once, to be a vehicle for power's oppression as well as a tool that has the potential to be wielded against such oppression. It also demonstrates how law's duality exists not just in its substantive provisions—the criminalizing power of Section 377 and the emancipatory potential of constitutional rights—but also in its technical and procedural norms. Early in the play, a witness resourcefully uses the threat of legal action against a homophobic therapist seeking to 'cure' her. But, as a lawyer tries to unsuccessfully explain to the court, it is the same threat of legal action that deters HIV-prevention work by non-governmental organizations.

This story is especially effective because it refracts these joyless debates through the lens of love. If what was at stake was the capacity to love, have India's LGBTQ people acquired that capacity because Section 377's criminalization of their identities has been vanquished? If not, was the two-decade-long effort by numerous persons to achieve this result pointless? What joy can India's sexual minorities experience in a new-found capacity to love at a time when its religious minorities are in the process of being deprived of that very right?

For all its imperfections, law is the best tool we have against power. Its victories over power are sometimes illusory, usually modest and incremental, often reversible, and never complete. At the end of *Love and Reparation*, a character asks another: 'How do you know there's going to be a next morning?'

We can only do as well as the reply to this question: 'I don't. I have no idea where this goes. Isn't that the fun part?'

Tarun Khaitan

Vice Dean, Faculty of Law, University of Oxford

15 March 2021

Practising Law, Practising Love

Instructions for living a life:
Pay attention.
Be astonished.
Tell about it.

Mary Oliver, 'Sometimes'

A perfectly insulated room in the student quarters at the University of Michigan Law School. December 2013: the first snowstorm in a winter that would be rife with them.

Midnight here in Ann Arbor; 10 a.m. in Delhi. I am feverishly scrolling across news sites while my study group skims through reading outlines. Any minute now, the Supreme Court of India will declare its verdict on the constitutional validity of Section 377 of the Indian Penal Code. Any minute now, the highest court of this country will decide if I am a criminal by virtue of being a gay man.

It has been 18 months since the final courtroom hearings in this matter. I've parsed the transcripts of those exchanges over and over. I was in the court through it all. I was there when a lawyer read a searing affidavit about a transgender woman's sexual assault in a police station. I was there when the judges impatiently asked him about the veracity of this claim. I have been in Ann Arbor for months now, but part of me is still in that courtroom.

10.30 a.m. in Delhi. The verdict is announced.

'We lost.' Tone flat with shock as I tell my classmates. The following morning, I walk in a daze to the planetarium and watch dotted points of light connecting in the sky map above me to form constellations. 'We lost.' The shock radiates from me in physical waves. This is heartbreak.

That day, I start writing *Contempt*, the first play in this volume.

✳

Courtroom No. 1, Supreme Court of India. September 2018: Delhi's monsoon humidity in full force.

Once again, the Court will declare its verdict on the constitutional validity of Section 377 of the Indian Penal Code. Victory feels like a foregone conclusion this time, but I did trick myself into that thought the last time and look what happened. Look at these past five years, fighting battles we thought we were done with. Let this be over.

The judges begin to speak. Thirty seconds in, we know it is over. Relief, I should feel relief, I do feel relief, but something else that doesn't lift. I walk out of the courtroom into an explosion of cameras and celebratory cheers. Later that night, at the biggest queer party this city has seen in a while, we dance. Bodies tangled, breaking apart. Air thick with glitter and sweat. A kiss of wine. *Freedom* they yell, *Freedom* ringing in my ears, so much freedom.

But I don't feel it in my body. Sweat on my arm that doesn't belong to me, smoke on my breath that isn't mine, a body, this body, that doesn't feel free.

That night, I start writing *Pride*, the second play in this volume.

✳

This is a fairly neat origin story, which also means it is somewhat inaccurate. Let me try again.

This is a book that brings together two plays about living with law. Because this is a law that regulated ways in which we love, these plays are also about how to love. About a life where law and love have been inseparably entwined.

I was thirteen when I first fell in love with a boy. I didn't realize it then. I only knew that I was willing to learn ninth-grade Sanskrit without any prior knowledge of the language just to be in a class with him.

I was sixteen when I fell in love with another boy. This time I knew what it was, this welter of joy and ache. I convinced myself it was a phase, a one-off kind of love.

I was seventeen when I first spoke the words that would slot the jigsaw confusion of the last six years into place. 'I'm gay,' I said, sitting in the dark, practising the utterance.

I was eighteen when I came across the text of the Indian Penal Code. 'Section 377: Unnatural Offences' it said in the index. I turned to the full text of the section and there it was, the description that the law had for the love I wanted so furiously: 'carnal intercourse against the order of nature'.

I was twenty-four when I sat in that room in wintry Ann Arbor as the Supreme Court of India delivered the *Suresh Kumar Koushal* judgement. I was a member of a minuscule minority, these judges said, too minuscule to overturn a law. The very possibility of some-one like me possessing constitutional rights seemed preposterous to these men: 'so-called rights' they called them. My shock and anger eventually wore off but these words lingered. They fed my shame, they enabled my tolerance of casual indignities in public, of casual cruelties in private.

Contempt was an attempt to come to terms with loss and anger and shame. A minor dissent, then.

I was twenty-nine when the highest constitutional court of my country declared that I was, unambiguously, an equal citizen. That I had, unambiguously, the right to love. It was done, it was done, it was over. Except it didn't feel like it was over, except that full sexual citizenship didn't magically whisk away the loss and anger and shame.

Pride was an attempt to come to terms with— what? This time around, the object of my dissent was less clear. All I knew was that I had to write my way through this tangle.

Or, perhaps, to wrought this tangle into shape.

*

Because isn't that what the playwright does?

Wright, as opposed to write. Wright as in a craftsperson, as in the one who builds and repairs. To wrought something is to ham-mer and melt and forge and craft.

Contempt is structured across four courtroom scenes. Each scene is forged from an unofficial transcription of the hearings that led to that first decision in 2013. The transcripts go on for a few hundred pages, reflecting six weeks of hearings. My reworking melted them down to four short scenes. I didn't need to alter any utterances made by the judges. John Berger once observed that graphic caricature is dead because life has outstripped it.

There is a peculiar privilege that playwrights have. With any luck—and I think I have had a lot of it—we wrought our work through watching our inchoate words performed. After one such reading with a group of trusted friends, two things became clear. One, the exchanges that transpired within the courtroom had a kind of awful but effective dramatic power, more so because of their basis in reality. Two, this reality wasn't enough. The play had to do more than restage a set of exchanges between judges and lawyers.

This is when the affidavits came in. Lawyers rely upon these documents to bridge the chasm between the institutional apparatus of law and the law as it is lived. A narration of experience becomes a certified truth that can be submitted before a court of law. How these stories are narrated is another question entirely. Look at most affidavits and you will see how they leach out the quotidian magic of everyday life. A life is stripped to the barest of facts, the most precise narrative constructed to provide evidence of harm. Somewhere in the production of evidence, the person behind the story disappears.

Contempt interleaves scenes in the courtroom with stories that I label affidavits. Each of these are accounts that begin with one foot planted in reality. From there, they meander, following imagined paths, resisting the neatness of the conventional legal affidavit.

One of these stories follows a character who is himself enamoured by stories. He opens the play with an account of a night of storytelling in ancient Greece. Later, he recasts that story within a contemporary moment, a fleeting encounter in an elevator. At points this character speaks like I do. Some of his experiences mirror mine. I don't necessarily think of this as memoir, but I do think it means that my learnings are his learnings. And vice versa.

Each time we recount a memory, each time we deliver a narration, it reconfigures our initial experience of the moment. That telling and retelling became one of the core themes of *Pride*. As the play begins, 377 is gone. Uber paths now appear on the app as rainbow-coloured trails. The fleeting elevator encounter of *Contempt* returns, this time within a conversation in therapy. Here is a man trying to figure something out: how to love in the aftermath of legality? He is surrounded by other people grappling with that aftermath: lawyers who stake a claim in the success of the case, queer persons who wonder how much of a landmark this is.

People who are impatient to move on, people who feel like they cannot let go. Matter decays at varying rates. Our bodies process variably. What is the half-life of law?

Pride does not rely on transcripts or legal texts for its framework except for a few key moments. I do like to think it is just as rooted in reality as *Contempt* is. And even though we barely enter a courtroom in this play, it is in equal measure a story about grappling with law. About coming to terms with law. About trying to craft a relationship of repair with it.

Trying to repair.

✳

Love and Reparation is the title of this book, the thing that gives it its shape. We sometimes use words before we've fully grasped their meaning or their relation to each other. I first came across these words, arranged in this manner, in the work of the psychoanalyst Melanie Klein. Let me set that scene for you; it feels important.

It is the summer of 2018 in London. I'm sitting in a park in Clapham, Jon awkwardly sprawled on the grass next to me. He is reading Klein's book of essays, pausing occasionally to complain about this uncomfortable reading environment or to quote dense chunks of prose at me. Clever Jon, a music composer who has somehow also inhaled a PhD's worth of psychoanalysis. He is telling me about Kleinian paranoid-schizoid and depressive positions but the ideas are difficult for me to grasp in their complexity. Later I will take the book from him and make some headway, but at that moment these words make, at best, a kind of intuitive sense.

This is not the first time Jon has challenged or surprised me. On our first date earlier that year, he gives me a copy of Paul Kalanithi's *When Breath Becomes Air*. Gifting a memoir about the life of a dying neurosurgeon to a person you've known for roughly three hours is a bit of a wild swing, but he takes it. The next day, he has me come over to a birthday gathering at a friend's house. A few hours in, he leans over.

Nice party but would you like to go do sex things now?

Of course, he is sitting across the room from me when he makes this proposition, six people watching this exchange.

Yes, obviously, I say, without skipping a beat.

I am visiting London from Delhi that week. *Contempt is* slated to open a theatre festival at the Arcola in Dalston. The plan is to attend the performance, have conversations around it, leave with ideas about how to produce the play in India. But then I meet Jon the day I land and every day after that, and as I leave for the airport, he sends me a screenshot from his attempts at googling the distance between our cities.

Why is it so far away?

It is far. Too far to keep minor conflicts from becoming insurmountable obstacles. Too far to eventually sustain a relationship. But not far enough to keep Jon from doing the work of alchemizing what we have into a nurturing friendship. On the street down from his therapist's office is a wall, graffitied with the following words: 'Let's adore and endure each other.' He thinks it is a perfect ethic. I think he embodies it.

Our conversations continue.

Jon's love of psychoanalysis infuses so many exchanges I have with him. On a video call, he holds a pillow wearing my shirt and tells me about transitional objects. That summer afternoon in Clapham, he tells me about love and reparation.

In her work, Klein identifies an anxiety that people first develop as infants—the anxiety of losing a love object. One way in which we deal with loss, with the possibility of it, is through practising a form of constant alertness. We might fall violently in love, and when love threatens to fail us, we raise the ramparts. The love object is poison; it must be cut off at all costs.

But it doesn't have to be all or nothing. We do not have to constantly prime ourselves for love's failure. We might also try and come to terms with the ambivalence of love. This is a melancholic realization, a moment where we open ourselves to pain and loss. It is also a moment where we have the chance to practise repair, to craft our love object into a source of nourishment.

✳

It is so hard to practise love, to practise repair. I can't think of anything more difficult than the struggle to first care for the self, and then somehow expand this radius to a circle of people around you. To do good by them, to nurture and care and help them grow.

Jon does it though. When we break, Jon finds a way to repair us. He doesn't give up on giving love, he doesn't give up on pushing me. Every conversation of ours is a challenge, a learning. It turns out, all of this is a rehearsal for a more demanding challenge.

Because then, Jon dies.

I'm sitting at my desk on the eighth floor of the Melbourne Law School when I receive the call. Four months into my PhD, trying to find different ways of approaching repair. It is 10 p.m. on the 22nd of November in London where his body lies; 11 a.m. in Melbourne on the 23rd. Many things become unfamiliar that day, my experience of time is one of them. Alive on the 22nd of November (my time). Dead on the 22nd of November (his time).

I walk out of the law-school building, get into the first tram I can find, ride it to the very last stop. I read his final text message to me, over and over. 'Ditch that pesky superego! Don't forget to fail a bit!'

We sometimes use words before we've fully grasped their meaning. Towards the end of *Contempt*, I gave a character a seemingly throwaway line: 'Pain has a vocabulary as varied as that of love.' It had a nice ring to it, it rounded off the scene in what felt like a satisfying manner. I thought I knew what it meant. But then Jon died and the knowledge of that loss unlocked a portal to a hidden world that ran just beneath the everyday one. *You want a vocabulary of pain? All right, there you go*—walk about gripping your jacket tighter because you are worried you will disperse into air or sit very very still for very very long to stop the spinning or ride yet another tram as far as it will go.

Solace arrives at unexpected moments, in unexpected places. I find myself attuning to wonder. I start to notice the gentle undulations of North Melbourne's terrain. I notice how alleyways empty out unbroken into slabs of glass and concrete that pierce the sky. I notice summer skies that explode with colour. I track the sky, so much sky, this vast expanse that opens up, so many colours to name, and start trying to name them—periwinkle, blush, teal, burnished copper, bluespark . . . on and on and on. As I name and notice, that griefswell, that painwelter does something too; it doesn't lessen but it shifts, flows so I can now watch it moving in and out and through me.

With enough practice, repair becomes an involuntary act.

*

As I write these words, it has been sixteen months since Jon died; two and a half years since the Supreme Court of India declared we were free; eight and a quarter years since a different bench of the court declared we were too minuscule a minority to deserve constitutional rights; nine years and a lifetime since a fleeting kiss in an elevator changed everything.

Each of these moments is lodged in my body.

The past is a thing that infiltrates, imbues, infuses the present—as Maria Tumarkin puts it.

The past lies in wait as an ambush—as Jeanette Winterson puts it.

Past is prologue. That's Shakespeare.

This week, I went to an exhibition at the Old Melbourne Gaol. The exhibit marks forty years of the decriminalization of homosexuality in the state of Victoria. Many of the queer people I know here will have lived their entire lives as legal citizens. That does not necessarily mean living outside the law's shadow. Too many stories of hate crimes, of police raids, of violence come after that defining moment of legal change.

But also within law's shadow are stories of people resisting, recrafting, reforging law into something nourishing. I am roughly halfway through a PhD where I've been trying to find ways of describing this practice. Academic writing, especially within the genre of the thesis, has its particular requirements: the demand to signpost and explain every strand of an argument, the necessity to trace your intellectual inheritance. There is a satisfying rigour to this. There is the sense of crafting what might just be a finished object, even if the object is ultimately the first rung on a very long ladder.

But you are not holding a thesis. This is a theatrical script. And theatrical scripts are never quite finished. They are inchoate words, forming an inchoate work. Theatre seems to demand more from a reader in this respect. Some might say too much—indeed, this is one of the reasons the drama sections in our local bookstores tend to be somewhat slender.

And yet, here we are somehow. You and I, in conversation.

Perhaps you will find that the inchoate nature of the theatrical script is also its affordance. Perhaps the theatrical form allows you more leeway to make the written world your own. That is my hope with this work, at any rate. I as writer, you as director, together we wrought. We can forge worlds, if we try.

And if you have read this far, perhaps you are willing to try? Perhaps you will take these words out for a walk, as I sometimes do. Perhaps on that walk, you will think with me, about what it means to seek and practice lawful love. About the ways in which shame seeps into our practice of it. About the ways in which the past haunts the everyday texture of it. About how we are haunted, whether legal citizenship arrived two years ago—or forty.

A NOTE ON SETTING

What follows is a highly attenuated timeline of the Section 377 litigation—an orienting device, of sorts. A short bibliographic essay in the closing pages of this book points you to a wealth of more detailed resources.

DECEMBER 2001: Naz Foundation, a non-governmental organization, files a petition challenging the constitutional validity of Section 377 of the Indian Penal Code in Delhi High Court. The section criminalizes 'carnal intercourse against the order of nature' and Naz Foundation argues that it must be struck down since it is used to target lesbian, gay, bisexual and transgender persons.

JULY 2009: A two-judge bench of the Delhi High Court delivers the *Naz Foundation v. Government of NCT of Delhi* judgement. It holds that Section 377 is unconstitutional 'since it denies a person's dignity and criminalises his or her core identity solely on account of his or her sexuality'. The following week, the decision is challenged by Suresh Kumar Koushal, an astrologer who files a petition against it before the Supreme Court of India.

FEBRUARY 2012: The Supreme Court of India hears the final arguments in the matter of *Suresh Kumar Koushal v. Naz Foundation*. The hearings take place over a six-week period.

Contempt **is based on these hearings.**

DECEMBER 2013: A two-judge bench of the Supreme Court delivers the *Suresh Kumar Koushal v. Naz Foundation* judgement. It reverses the Delhi High Court decision and holds that Section 377 of the Indian Penal Code is constitutional. Once again, queer persons in India are criminalized.

2014: A range of petitions are filed before the Supreme Court, challenging the validity of *Suresh Kumar Koushal v. Naz Foundation*. The Court agrees to hear them before a larger bench but does not set a date for hearings.

2016: On the basis of a petition filed by the dancer Navtej Singh Johar along with five other individuals who argue they are all directly aggrieved by Section 377, the Supreme Court agrees to constitute a five-judge bench to hear the matter. The matter is eventually listed for hearing in 2018.

JULY 2018: The Supreme Court of India hears the final arguments in the matter of *Navtej Singh Johar v. Union of India*. The hearings take place over a one-week period.

SEPTEMBER 2018: A five-judge bench of the Supreme Court delivers the *Navtej Singh Johar v. Union of India* judgement. It reverses the *Suresh Kumar Koushal* decision and effectively decriminalizes queer intimacy in private between consenting adults in India.

Pride **is written in the aftermath of this decision.**

PART I

CONTEMPT

CHARACTERS

JUDGE 1: Male, 40s to 60s

JUDGE 2: Male, 40s to 60s

LAWYER: Male, mid to late 40s

WITNESS 1: Male, mid 20s to early 30s

WITNESS 2: Female, mid 20s to early 30s

WITNESS 3: Female, early to mid 20s

WITNESS 4: Transgender woman, 30s

The judges will be seated within the audience from the start of the play and remain there for its duration. There are five chairs on the stage, placed at regular intervals. When the play opens, Witness 1 is seated on the chair in the centre. The lawyer, when he is onstage, stands behind this central chair.

WITNESS 1

I—love—you.

I love you.

These words come way too easily to me. So I go on a date with this guy, second date, he picks one of those *Time Out*–featured restaurants, orders the second-cheapest wine on the menu, doesn't check his phone more than once in the evening, is reasonably non-disappointing in bed and then—the next morning—offers to make coffee.

And that's it, that's all it takes, and it just comes tumbling right out: thanks-for the-coffee-I-love-you!

And then of course he looks all horrified and goes stumbling out of the house before I can explain that I really meant to say love with a small *l*—like font size 7—like the Outer Ring Road of love.

You know who got this? The Greeks.

The ancient Greeks, they understood the big difference between the I-love-you-s of good sex and the I-love-you-s that lead to joint tax declarations.

They knew that no one word could capture the infinite messiness of love, and so they had several. Ludus—playful love. Pragma—longstanding love. Philia—love of the mind. Agape—love of the soul. Storge—love of the child. Philautia—love of the self . . . and then.

And then, there was another kind of love. A love rooted in erotic frenzy, a love that could shatter worlds. Eros, that's what they called it, and one night, thousands of years ago, a group of men gathered together in ancient Greece to honour eros.

There were eight of them that night at the house of Agathon. The tables groaned with food and goblets of wine. A gentle music serenaded them as the summer-night breeze wafted through the room, plucking beads of sweat glistening on their uncovered bodies.

There were eight of them.

A statesman, a doctor, a playwright, a poet, a philosopher, a lawyer. Outside the door of the house, there was another man listening, waiting, hoping. His name was Alcibiades, but he's not important just yet. For now, it's these men, getting drunk and delivering odes to the glory, the magnificence of eros. They tell us how eros is mania, how it is poetry, how it is medicine for the soul, how it is a quest for the other half of the soul. They agree that eros is crucial, that it is vital.

And finally, they come to Socrates. Who of course must have the last word, because he is Socrates the great, Socrates the father of Western philosophy. And he says, Well, eros, eh. Eros is fine, eros is good. But really, let's do away with the carnal pleasures of the flesh. Let's do away this eros, lets climb the ladder of beauty. Let's move towards a higher good.

Let's reject eros.

Witness 1 walks offstage; Lawyer enters.

ROUND I

THIS COLONIAL LEGACY

LAWYER. Your lordships, I stand before you today in the matter of *Suresh Kumar Koushal v. Naz Foundation*. This is a matter that affects the lives of millions of citizens in our country. We argue that Section 377 of the Indian Penal Code is unconstitutional, that it criminalizes the intimate lives of lesbian, gay, bisexual, transgender individuals in the country, that it exposes them to harassment, blackmail, persecution, prosecution. In 2009 the Delhi High Court held that it does violate the Constitution, that as far as two adults who have consensual sexual intercourse in private are concerned, they should not, they cannot be criminalized under the law—

JUDGE 1. So the question before us is whether the Delhi High Court judgement is correct or not.

LAWYER. I respectfully submit your lordships that the question is broader, and it is one that is stated in the petition.

JUDGE 2. And can you formulate that for us, counsel?

LAWYER. Your lordships, the question is whether Section 377 of the Indian Penal Code, as it is interpreted today, is violative of Articles 14, 15 and 21 of the Constitution. We thus do not ask you to merely consider whether the Delhi High Court was wrong or right though we do stand by their judgement. What we are submitting before you is to consider this matter afresh, and in so doing to find that Section 377 does in fact violate the

6

constitutional rights to equality, non-discrimination, health, privacy and personal liberty. We place before you a number of documents and affidavits to show that there is widespread abuse of the section, which leads to harassment faced by LGBT individuals—

JUDGE 1. We want to clarify, counsel, whether this is a finding of the High Court or the perception of individuals?

LAWYER. Lordship, I'm not sure I understand.

JUDGE 1. When 377 is abused—is that a general issue that happens with the law, is there a specific finding of abuse with respect to LGBT—is there clear documentation of their being targeted— or is it misused in the way that other provisions of the law are misused. Can we just give a general declaration about the law?

LAWYER. A general declaration—yes, your lordship. You would not say that it is reasonable for Section 377 to be applied to a husband and wife. You would draw the line there. We are asking for the line to be drawn at consensual sex between any adults in private, which would then stop the law from being misused against LGBT persons.

JUDGE 1. Please read Section 377 for us.

LAWYER. 'Whoever has carnal intercourse against the order of nature, with man, woman or animal shall be punished with imprisonment for a term . . .'

JUDGE 1. Whoever!

JUDGE 2. Whoever. Who-so-ever.

JUDGE 1. Counsel, tell us where is the mention of lesbians, gays, etc. here?

LAWYER. They aren't explicitly mentioned, your lordship, but we have overwhelming evidence to show over the past 150 years that it is LGBT persons who have been targeted under this law.

JUDGE 1. Overwhelming!

JUDGE 1. Counsel. If the law is silent on this LGBT question, then how is it that you are making this argument, how is it that only LGBT are being chased under the law?

LAWYER. Your lordships, I am telling you that this was the intent of the law, and that these are the people who the law was originally created to persecute.

JUDGE 2. But how do we know this?

LAWYER. By looking at the origin of the law. By looking at how it has made its way into the Indian Penal Code. Your lordships, if we go back in time, the first recorded mention of sodomy in English law was in two medieval texts that prescribed that sodomites should be burnt alive. Then, when secular laws began to come into place in England, you had the Buggery Act in the sixteenth century—

JUDGE 2. Counsel, where are we?

LAWYER. In the Supreme Court, your lordships.

JUDGE 2. Yes, and where is the Supreme Court?

LAWYER. We are on Tilak Marg . . .

JUDGE 2. No I mean what country is the court in?

LAWYER. India, your lordships.

JUDGE 1. Exactly. India. Why are we concerned with what happened in England in the sixteenth century?

JUDGE 2. Are we in England?

LAWYER. No lordships, there is little doubt that we're in India. I'm only trying to tell you where this law comes from and explain to you that the historical context will help us understand why it is that specific terms like gay or lesbian are not used in the law—

JUDGE 1. We don't need a history class, counsel. This is a court of law. You just tell us what this law means.

LAWYER. Absolutely, your lordships, and the best way to understand what this means and who this covers is to place it in its context, and see that it was intended to cover the act of homosexual sodomy. Except that the British were so concerned about not naming the identity, about not drawing people's attention to this particular social group that they said, and I quote: 'We are unwilling to insert in the text anything which could give rise to public discussion on this revolting subject—'

JUDGE 2. Speaking of inserting, counsel, please go back to this carnal intercourse question.

LAWYER. Yes, your lordships, the point is that this term has been used in reference to LGBT individuals—

JUDGE 1. Counsel, counsel, where are you getting this from!?

LAWYER. As I mentioned, the British referenced a revolting subject—

JUDGE 1. But there are so many revolting subjects!

JUDGE 2. How do we know exactly what the revolting subject was?

JUDGE 1. Yes, how do we know exactly what this carnal intercourse against the order of nature is? What acts are being targeted?

LAWYER. But your, lordships, that's why the context is important, that's why history is important—we need to see that this was never about specific acts, it's about the groups that they refer to—

JUDGE 2. That is not what the section says.

JUDGE 1. The section is clear. It says: Carnal. Intercourse. Against. The. Order. Of. Nature.

Witness 2 enters and takes a seat on stage. Lawyer exits.

WITNESS 2

My dad's all about the big declarations. When I was in the tenth grade, he needed to tell me just how proud he was about my board-exam results. Instead of using his words like regular people do, he waits till we're on a flight a week afterwards. So here we are, settling in, when the pilot informs us in case we're confused, that we're flying to Bangalore, that the flying time will be two hours and twenty minutes, some turbulence expected but he wishes us a comfortable journey. Then a pause, and in a very different tone, still on the intercom, still within earshot of all those other passengers, he wishes the young genius girl in seat 12A (*gesticulates at herself*) a huge round of applause for her board exam results.

It was a . . . long ride for young genius.

Seven years later, young genius girl became young genius woman and told her parents she was lesbian. Or, well, let them find it out anyway. My attempts at the heterosexual exams did not go quite as well as my boards—I was a miserable failure at being straight and even worse at being closeted. The conversation took place over the phone. There were tears, recriminations, and then silence. Finally, in a broken voice, Dad said, just come home. Just for the weekend.

And so I do. Mum picks me up from the airport, and I let the car ride pass in silence, only speaking up when I see that we've taken the wrong lane. But she shakes her head at the driver. It isn't a wrong turn. We are driving, I would find out, directly to the office of the friendly neighbourhood psychiatrist.

I say nothing, I do nothing, I let this fact seep into me, I will be calm, I will be a good young genius lesbian who deals with her forced psychiatric visits with fortitude. As we walk into the lobby, I see my father's already there and I flash him my most beatific smile. He looks as confused as I feel terrified.

As I'm ushered into the good doctor's room, my parents take a seat on either side of me. Doc surveys me wordlessly for a few seconds, I look wordlessly back, maybe this is the first test, a staring contest. Then he tilts his head sideways, and leans forward:

(*At this point, the psychologist's lines are to be delivered alternately by Judges 1 and 2.*)

'Do you know why you're here?'

Instead of answering, I decide to continue playing the wordless staring game. That seems so much more fun.

'You're here because you're homosexual.'

I attempt to look confused, as if he's spoken a difficult French word.

'How do you feel about being homosexual?'

At this, I break my silence: 'Oh I'm actually quite happy about being lesbian.'

He flinches at the word lesbian like a vampire confronted with the Delhi sun but continues valiantly: 'So you're saying you're fine with being homosexual?'

Before I can get to playing the semantics game, he indicates in my mother's directions and asks me, 'Well, so if she commits suicide because of you, that's fine, is it?'

'You know, two can play at that game', the words have left my mouth before I realize what I've said—there is a mildly convulsive moment from either side of me, but I cannot acknowledge them, it is between me and the doctor now.

He gets down to brass tacks. 'Look, there are three ways in which we can approach this condition. One, homosexuality might be caused by hormonal imbalances. Two, it could be a result of some tumour in the brain. And three, it could be caused by some other mental disorder.'

I take a moment to let these words sink in. I have a choice here. I can listen quietly and brush it off, no big deal, screw him. *Or* I can make a big scene about this, and really screw him.

I have a choice.

I choose drama.

I take out my phone, place it on the table, and tell him: 'Just so you know, I've recorded this entire conversation. And you look confused (and good god he does, he looks gloriously baffled) so let me tell you why I've done that. I'm going to use this as evidence for the FIR I file against you the moment I walk out of this office.'

It pays off almost instantly, and for the first time since we walk into his room, his smug smile wavers. 'What would you do that for?'

'Well, to begin with,' I tell him, 'I'm going to have you booked for medical malpractice and causing emotional distress. You have all these huge certificates and medals in your office but it doesn't look like you know that the WHO removed homosexuality from its International Classification of Diseases in 1990. Calling it a mental disorder is practising incorrect medicine, how can you not know this? Or else, you knew this and still decided to pull off this nonsense. Ah! You know what, that's going to make an even better case, thank you, thank you so much.'

This is a moment where I fear the inconveniently loud thud of my heart will betray me, but he jumps the panic gun first, looking to my parents: 'It's clear she's suffering from some form of paranoid schizophrenia, we might need some instant aggressive treatment!'

But I've had enough at this point.

I get up and storm out of the room, ignoring the yells, run to the first auto-rickshaw I can find, a straight dash to the airport, oblivious to the insistent buzzing of my phone, unaware that I've left my suitcase back in the car. I run to the ticketing counter in a daze, buy the first ride back to Delhi, another dash past security, and now down the boarding line. The trance breaks when I am finally seated in the plane and the pilot begins his announcement. He informs us, in case we are confused, that we are flying to Delhi and that the flying time will be an hour and twenty minutes, and that we have clear skies ahead.

There are no further announcements. We take off into the night.

Witness 2 remains seated; Lawyer re-enters.

ROUND II
WHAT GOES WHERE?

LAWYER. Your lordships, I stand before you today in the matter of *Suresh Kumar Koushal v. Naz Foundation*, a matter that affects the lives of millions of citizens in our country. We argue that Section 377 of the Indian Penal Code is unconstitutional, that it criminalizes the intimate lives of lesbian, gay, bisexual, transgender individuals in the country—

JUDGE 1. How exactly?

LAWYER. My lordships, I represent a group of individuals who find that the law violates their basic fundamental rights guaranteed under the Constitution. Our argument is that the section singles out one set of persons—the LGBT population—and holds them criminals for exercising their sexuality.

JUDGE 2. But how does it do that?

LAWYER. Because, your lordships, it is used to specifically persecute LGBT persons and no other group, and so it treats them differently from the general population. In doing so, their constitutional right to equality and non-discrimination is violated.

JUDGE 1. That's not what my brother judge asked you, counsel.

JUDGE 2. No, counsel, tell us, why are you talking about lesbian, gay—why are you talking about these people in this case?

LAWYER. My lordships, it is precisely these individuals who are targeted under Section 377—

JUDGE 2. Counsel, who is this Naz Foundation?

LAWYER. Lordship, it is an NGO that works on HIV/AIDS—

JUDGE 1. Why do they care about LGBT?

LAWYER. They work with communities that are particularly vulnerable to HIV/AIDS transmission, and men who have sex with men are amongst these communities.

JUDGE 1. So they should focus on their work. Why are they coming here?

LAWYER. Because, your lordship, when you criminalize certain sexual acts as 377 does, you make it very difficult to provide HIV prevention programmes relating to those acts and this impacts the constitutional right to health.

JUDGE 2. And how exactly is that?

LAWYER. Your lordships, think of how HIV prevention programmes work. The organization employs healthcare workers to go to the field, and talk to people about safe-sex practices and distribute pamphlets and condoms to them.

JUDGE 1. So who is stopping them, counsel?

LAWYER. The police is, your lordships. A lot of the ground staff of these organizations get harassed and picked up by the police for encouraging what the police say is immoral and illegal activity.

JUDGE 2. And?

LAWYER. And so, you see, organizations that do crucial work like this, that are helping to stop the spread of HIV/AIDS, cannot do their work effectively because of the existence of Section 377.

There is a pause. The judges confer among themselves.

JUDGE 1. Counsel, tell us something. How is this NGO funded?

LAWYER. Your lordship?

JUDGE 2. It is quite clear what my brother judge asked. How does this NGO receive funds? Are they foreign funds?

JUDGE 1. How much foreign funding?

LAWYER. Lordships this is not about where the NGO's money is coming from—

JUDGE 2. Yes, but the NGO is making this argument so we need to see who is behind this argument.

LAWYER. The government is behind this argument your lordship, NACO—the National Aids Control Organization has stated exactly the same thing.

JUDGE 1. Actually, where is NACO getting its funding from?

LAWYER. Lordships . . .

JUDGE 2. OK fine, OK fine, you forget all that. Forget all this HIV. Tell us, what does Section 377 actually say?

LAWYER. Whoever has carnal intercourse against the order of nature—

JUDGE 1. Carnal intercourse—

JUDGE 2. Against the order of nature—

LAWYER. That is correct, and it applies—

JUDGE 1. Wait. Tell us this, what is this carnal intercourse against the order of nature?

LAWYER. If we are to look at how it has been interpreted by the appellate courts, along with a historical reading of the section, it's abundantly clear that it targets sexual acts done by LGBT individuals.

JUDGE 2. It's clear?

JUDGE 1. Abundantly clear?

LAWYER. It has been overwhelmingly used to—

JUDGE 1. Doesn't seem clear to us.

JUDGE 2. What is this order of nature?

LAWYER. Lordships, sexual or carnal intercourse within the order of nature would ordinarily refer to a situation where sex can result in the possibility of reproduction.

JUDGE 1. So penile-vaginal sex?

LAWYER. Essentially yes, your lordship. So even the use of contraceptives would technically be against the order of nature.

JUDGE 2. So then this section covers everyone?

LAWYER. If we are to just read it as it is, yes, but we have to take into account the question of how it's been used—

JUDGE 1. But counsel, we don't have an authoritative definition of order of nature. What is this carnal intercourse against the order of nature? What kinds of sexual acts are against the order of nature?

LAWYER. We don't have a specific list of acts—

JUDGE 2. What if . . . a boy inserts his tongue into another's mouth?

JUDGE 1. What if . . . a father inserted his tongue while kissing his child?

JUDGE 2. What about . . . the breast of a mother and child?

JUDGE 1. A mother puts her fist in the mouth of her child—

LAWYER. Your lordships, it isn't a question of what acts, it's a question of which identities are targeted by this vague set of acts, it's a question of how LGBT individuals are associated with whatever acts are considered to be covered under Section 377, and that they are disproportionately impacted as a result of that.

(*A beat*)

It just isn't about the acts, it is about identities.

Pause. Perhaps this idea has finally connected with the Judges.

JUDGE 1 (*continues as if the lawyer hasn't said anything, clicks his finger in glee having come up with a great example*). But what about when one person hugs another person very tightly? Could that be carnal intercourse against the order of nature?

Witness 3 enters and takes a seat on stage; Lawyer exits.

WITNESS 3

AFFIDAVIT 8107/2012

I have known Swapna since the time I knew that fire could hurt you.

We are ten and walking to school together. I am half a pace behind her, claiming each of her footprints as mine. We are one unit and they know it and see it before we do—look here come Swapna–Sucheta.

We are twelve and she is home giving me maths tuitions but I am not that bad and she is not that good but she is giving me tuitions anyway because then after the tuitions she can stay with me and then we lie together at night, talking, confirming each event for each other, because what she sees I might see but it is always transformed by how she sees it and I want to know every last detail. Our conversations repeat themselves endlessly, but even that observation becomes another conversation and we talk and talk ourselves to sleep.

We are fifteen and sharing a mango and she slices it tenderly and she gives me a slice, the big slice, but her generosity is lost on me, I can only see that when she bites into the flesh a thin line of the juice races down her chin, and past her throat, thin defiant streak of orange disappearing into crisp white blouse. She is gazing at a point in the distance, and I think how generous is my Swapna, she is letting me gaze undisturbed. I do not realize then how she takes just as much pleasure from me looking at her.

We are seventeen and she still gives me tuitions and this is just another night after just another tuition but this night we play a game where she traces equations on my arm, such is my teacher, and then she traces her name on my navel and we giggle at first but then she moves her finger down and I can't laugh and she moves further down and all I can do is move closer and let her disappear into me.

We are nineteen and she is home with me when the first boy's family comes to visit. She walks me with such confidence to the room they are sitting in, she even makes the tea for him and he asks shyly if she is my sister. That becomes our joke, later that night when we lie together and she whispers 'sister, dear sweet sister' into the nape of my neck.

And now we are twenty and our stories are coming to an end. I cannot be sure when it was clear we were on borrowed time, but we both knew at the same moment. She came to my house that night though there were no tuition excuses left, but no one asked, no one suspected. And when it came to it, in those final moments, we didn't cry. It isn't that we were being brave for each other. We were sure that this would be just another conversation where we'd fall asleep and then wake up and find each other again.

When they find our bodies, they will see them tied together with a piece of cloth around our waists. We thought that would help. We asked for our bodies to be kept in the same place, together for all time, like we used to be, and we thought that the cloth would help, we thought it would remind them of how much this final request meant to us.

It may not matter to them or to you, but it is what we wanted in the end, and that should be enough. It should.

Witness 3 remains seated; Lawyer re-enters.

ROUND III
KOKILA SPEAKS

LAWYER. Your lordships, I stand before you today in the matter of *Suresh Kumar Koushal v. Naz Foundation*, a matter that affects the lives of millions of citizens in our country. We argue that Section 377 of the Indian Penal Code is unconstitutional—

JUDGE 1. How, counsel? How are these millions of citizens affected?

LAWYER. If you will permit me, I would like to read out an affidavit to you. This is by Kokila, a hijra woman from Bangalore. It has been admitted into the court record.

At the mention of Kokila, Witness 4 walks onstage and takes a seat.

LAWYER. My name is Kokila. I identify myself as a hijra, that is a member of a traditional male-to-female transsexual community in South Asia. Right from my childhood, I have felt that I was a girl and liked to dress in girls' clothes, cook and put on make-up.

Witness 4 now speaks instead of the Lawyer.

WITNESS 4. On the 18th of June 2004 around 8 p.m., while I was dressed in women's clothing and waiting on the road, I was raped by ten men who forcefully took me to the grounds next to Old Madras Road.

JUDGE 1. Now, counsel—

WITNESS 4. They threatened to kill me if I wouldn't have sex with them. I was forced to have oral and anal sex with all of them. While I was being sexually assaulted, two policemen arrived and the men ran away. I told them about the sexual assault by the goondas.

JUDGE 2. But what about—

WITNESS 4. Instead of registering a case against the goondas and sending me for medical examination, they harassed me with offensive language and took me along with the two captured goondas to the Byappanahalli Police Station.

JUDGE 1. And why—

WITNESS 4. The police did not even allow me to put on my trousers and forced me to be naked for the next seven hours. In the station, I was subjected to brutal torture, I was stripped, naked, my hands handcuffed to a window. They hit me with their lathis, they kicked me with their boots, they abused me using sexually violent language, they burnt my nipples with a burning coir rope.

The judges confer. Witness 4 sits silently, looking at the judges.

JUDGE 2. Counsel, one question: How do we know this happened?

Witness 4 and the Lawyer look at each other, their faces impassive. The lawyer breaks the gaze after a few beats and looks back at the Judges.

LAWYER. Your lordship, as mentioned, I am reading from an affidavit, made under oath, on penalty of perjury.

JUDGE 1. Yes, but is there any other evidence that this event happened?

LAWYER. There are multiple newspaper accounts and fact-finding reports which I can produce before you corroborating the events Kokila describes.

JUDGE 1. But do these reports talk about how this is a case about 377?

LAWYER. As you can see, Section 377 creates a situation where these abuses can happen. It legitimizes this behaviour.

JUDGE 1. Counsel, how does it do that—

JUDGE 2. From what we have understood, it criminalizes carnal intercourse against the order of nature—

JUDGE 1. Are these instances of carnal intercourse against the order of nature?

A beat, lawyer is silent, looks at them intently. He leaves the stage.

WITNESS 4

My name is Kokila. Kokila means cuckoo. This is not the name on my birth certificate. I will not tell you what that name is. It is not mine.

My name is Kokila. My parents use it to call me now. It took some time, but they use it. After all, there is nothing else I will answer to.

My name is Kokila. I cannot remember how long I have known this, or when I realized it. I think I heard it first in a bus.

My name is Kokila. When we are lying in bed, I make him whisper it to me as I am falling asleep, maybe I am scared he will forget otherwise. When he leaves in the morning, I make him repeat it. Don't say bye, don't say bye my love. Say bye Kokila, say it, say it again, bye Kokila, say it like that, yes. It means cuckoo, did I mention that? I don't know what cuckoo birds are really like, or if I am at all like a cuckoo, but when you say it to me it is the right sound.

My name is Kokila, Kokila *is* my name. They don't believe it. When I try to make them write it in black ink on green paper with a blue stamp, they look at me like I have come to the wrong place. But there is one document that calls me Kokila. There is one place where you will say it, there is one place where you will allow me to say who I am, that I exist. It is an affidavit. It speaks about my rape.

My name is Kokila. If you repeat a word enough times, it loses its meaning.

I would still very much like you to say my name.

Witness 4 remains seated; Lawyer re-enters.

ROUND IV
ON MIRRORS

LAWYER. Your lordships, I stand before you today in the matter of *Suresh Kumar Koushal v. Naz Foundation*, a matter that affects the lives of millions—

JUDGE 1. In what way?

JUDGE 2. Where in this Section 377 does it actually say—

LAWYER (*raises his voice, cuts off the judge*). The point here, your lordships, is that this is *not* a case about who does what acts.

JUDGE 1. Then what—

LAWYER (*voice raised even higher, cuts off judge again*). If we can just take a step back, away from the specific words of this law, and see what is it that it actually allows for. What does it mean for a person who is gay, lesbian, bisexual, transgender? What does it mean for them to wake up in the morning and look in the mirror, and see a criminal, to see an unapprehended felon, to see themselves stripped of their dignity.

JUDGE 1. But who are these people? Where do we find them?

LAWYER. Lordship, we don't have to find them, it's not about how we identify them, it's about how they identify themselves—how they view themselves—which is, as second-class citizens under the law. Being criminalized affects their right to dignity—

JUDGE 2. Can they be identified?

LAWYER. As I said—

JUDGE 2. If they can't be identified as such how is their dignity affected? Harassment can only happen if a person can be identified

LAWYER. The norm is such that many individuals cannot come out, they cannot be open about their sexuality

JUDGE 1. Of course you can, provided you have access to the media—then you will be glorified!

JUDGE 2. And otherwise, why do they have to be out like that? Who walks around saying, 'I am a heterosexual, I am a heterosexual?'

JUDGE 1. Exactly, dignity can only be compromised if your identity is revealed.

LAWYER. But, your lordships, we cannot ask people to hide their sexuality, whether it is visible or not. The point is this law means that you cannot express aspects of your sexuality—

JUDGE 1. That applies to everyone.

LAWYER. But for the others, for those who don't belong to the LGBT community, there is a way of expressing their sexuality that is considered within the order of nature, that is not condemned!

JUDGE 2 (*highly irritable now*): Community community community—what is this community?

JUDGE 1. Yes, this community business, doesn't your argument also extend to someone attracted to animals only?

JUDGE 2. Someone will say, I am attracted to animals, only now you protect my dignity.

LAWYER. That . . . that's a very . . . different situation, my lord, we're not on that . . .

JUDGE 1. Let me tell you there was this peculiar incident in Punjab. These three ladies were frequent pickpockets. One Robin Hood SP got hold of them and got tattoos engraved on their foreheads to mark them as pickpockets. Now will we also call them a community?

LAWYER. That . . . your lordship . . .

JUDGE 2. You are making arguments that are contradictory—how can dignity be compromised if people don't know your identity?

JUDGE 1. There doesn't have to be a special community. People are part of the general commune.

LAWYER. But it is this general community, this larger community that has decided that LGBT people are criminals in the first place. Section 377 reflects the will of the community, it reflects popular sentiment, popular morality, and that is precisely the problem your lordships.

(*He utters the next words slowly, hoping for the weight of each to land before the Court.*)

Our test has to be that of constitutional morality, not popular morality. Our test has to be that of the values identified by the Constitution, the values we agreed to be constituted by as a nation—*not* those of popular sentiment.

JUDGE 2. But why should the law change this, opinions should be changed through other ways—

LAWYER. Your lordships, at the time our Constitution was being drafted, B. R. Ambedkar said that constitutional morality was not a natural sentiment. It has to be cultivated, it has to be fostered on a top-soil that is essentially anti-democratic, it does not come to people naturally—

JUDGE 1. Speaking of natural, if you do natural acts, then you won't be a criminal!

LAWYER (*visibly exasperated, but continues after a breath*). But that is the problem, how do you define what is natural and what is normal?

JUDGE 1. Exactly, then, what is natural? What is normal?

JUDGE 2. What is this carnal intercourse against the order of nature?

LAWYER. *You* can decide this, my lordships—*you* can say that there is nothing unnatural about sexual acts by LGBT individuals, that they are not against the order of nature . . .

JUDGE 2. But which acts? Where is that in your pleadings? You say homosexuals are not unnatural—but which acts?

JUDGE 1. What about . . . hugging?

Lawyer at this point has frozen in silence.

JUDGE 2. What about when a father puts his tongue—

JUDGE 1. What about when a mother feeds her child—

JUDGE 2. Actually, hold on, counsel, this is just not working, tell us one thing. Why are you here?

JUDGE 1. Yes, what is really your cause of action?

LAWYER. Why are we here . . .

JUDGE 1. Yes, counsel.

JUDGE 2. Yes—why?

LAWYER (*after a long pause as he looks at both judges*). I don't think I know any more.

JUDGE 2. What kind of an answer—

LAWYER. I don't know.

JUDGE 1. Counsel!

LAWYER. I do not know.

JUDGE 2. Counsel, are you mocking us?

LAWYER. Mocking? Not mocking, no.

JUDGE 1. Counsel, we will have to hold you in contempt!

Lawyer gives a sigh of resignation, looks up with a wry smile.

LAWYER. Contempt? (*In a monotonous voice as if reciting from a statute book*) Contempt. Whoever makes a statement which lowers the authority of the court will be held in contempt.

JUDGE 2. We know what the definition of contempt is, counsel.

LAWYER. And yet. (*A laugh, a shrug, a nod. He takes a seat onstage.*)

Before he can say anything else, Witness 1 speaks from behind the audience. As he continues to speak, he makes his way onto the stage.

And yet.

I need you to understand.

No wait. Understand—not understand—that isn't the right word, not for me anyway. *He*—he would use it, he would say it because to understand is to rationalize and think with reason and reason is good, and has its uses but reason will only take us so far, and here reason fails us.

So no, not understand. I need to take you . . . there.

I need to take you to this night that changed everything. Except, it's really two nights. The first is the night of the *Symposium*. The night when Socrates tells us we must do away with the carnal pleasures of the flesh, down with eros! And as he says it all these men of Athens around him applaud, oh, Socrates, you great, smart man, doing away with eros, revolutionary!

And then, at this celebratory moment, in walks Alcibiades.

Young, brash, inflamed by passion, Alcibiades. Crazed former lover of Socrates, Alcibiades. Alcibiades who tells us about how he has ached for Socrates only to be slowly destroyed in his breathless pursuit of this man, this man who casually makes him burn with love, and then, even more casually denies him. You want to talk about eros, he says? I'll tell you about eros.

Eros is not pleasant. It is not beautiful. It grates you out of existence. It is sweet-bitter, this eros, it is pain, it is pleasure, it is both and it is neither all at once. And every conversation we have, my

Socrates and I, every single moment we spend together is a moment caught in that in-between space. Will you still deny eros? Will you still deny me?

But Socrates does deny him. And that story ends there.

Which brings me to the second night. Thousands of years later, there was a night in 2012, a night where once again, eight of us are seated on a table, this time on a rooftop, getting drunk and talking about love. This night . . . I am seated here, at this edge . . . and diagonally across is my own flesh-and-blood tormentor, the subject of my breathless pursuit, my very own Socrates.

Witness 1 takes the final remaining seat on stage. He looks at the Lawyer, who returns his gaze.

LAWYER. Can you see us, seated around a table, insulated from the wintry night by steady intoxication and conversations about love?

WITNESS 1. Can you see us, and remember that we are sitting diagonally opposite each other?

LAWYER. Can you think of how the occasional wordless glance might hit with a physical force as the evening progresses?

WITNESS 1. And in the air, can you sense it, that manic, hovering force apprised of its targets, eros itself, about to latch on any second now?

LAWYER. And now the wine is over—

WITNESS 1. And now conversations have come to a close—

LAWYER. And now eight of us walk to the elevator—

WITNESS 1. Eight, to an elevator that can hold only six in one go—

LAWYER. And of all the permutations and combinations—

WITNESS 1. All the ways we could have arranged ourselves—

LAWYER. The six that walk into the elevator do not include you and me—

WITNESS 1. And so the others go ahead—

LAWYER. The others go ahead—

WITNESS 1. The others go ahead . . . and . . .

LAWYER. . . . . And we stand next to each other in silence.

WITNESS 1. And then the door opens and you walk inside first.

LAWYER. And you follow, your back turned to me

And now the other Witnesses join in so they all alternate lines with one another.

WITNESS 4. Even before the door closes, I feel your breath on my neck. Mere inches separate us.

WITNESS 3. One floor down, you take the faintest of steps backward, now my breath is stronger, and we are so close that I can feel the heat radiate from your body.

WITNESS 2. Another floor down, I turn around to look at you, our proximity makes our noses brush, we are both looking at the ground. The air that separates the rest of our bodies from contact is surely, surely on fire.

WITNESS 4. Another floor down, this thin fire becomes cold sweat, we are immobile and trembling, and then the elevator comes to a halt.

WITNESS 2. And here, the door could have opened to show us every-body waiting outside, but they aren't there . . . and it could have opened to strangers waiting to use the elevator but there is no one else either.

WITNESS 3. And so of course it makes all the sense in the world when you reach from behind and push the button for the fifth floor once again. For the second time, the doors close on us.

LAWYER. And . . .

WITNESS 1. And . . .

As the Judges interrupt this moment, Witness 1 and the Lawyer look away from each other.

JUDGE 1. In the matter of *Suresh Kumar Koushal v. Naz Foundation*, we find that a minuscule fraction of the country's population includes lesbians, gays, bisexuals and transgenders.

JUDGE 2. That Section 377 does not violate the so-called rights of the LGBT community.

JUDGE 1. And we therefore hold that Section 377 of the Indian Penal Code does not violate the Constitution of India.

A pause. A long pause, as we sit with the weight of these words.

And then, slowly, Witness 1 and the Lawyer turn around to face each other.

A defiant smile spreads across their faces.

LAWYER. And . . .

WITNESS 1. And . . .

WITNESS 4. You kiss me, like it will be the only kiss we will ever have.

WITNESS 3. You kiss me. Like we are discovering something new.

WITNESS 2. You kiss me. And I marvel at how your breath becomes my air.

WITNESS 1. And you kiss me. And there will be more as the evening passes. There will be time. Years perhaps. And then I will lose you, Socrates, and I will learn that pain has a vocabulary as varied as that of love. But for now, for this moment, will you stay in this elevator with me? Can you see the two of us, dissolving into each other that night? Can you see how this was the most beautiful thing—the most crucial thing in the world? Can you see why beauty is important? Can you see why it is crucial?

LAWYER. Can you?

Performance of *Contempt* at Oddbird Theatre, Delhi, 3 June 2018. Photograph by Prateeq Kumar. *Reproduced with the photographer's permission.*

PART II

PRIDE

CHARACTERS

A: Male, late 20s to early 30s

T: Female, mid to late 50s

PERSON 1: Male, mid to late 40s

PERSON 2: Female, mid 30s to late 40s

PERSON 3: Male, late 20s to early 30s

PERSON 4: Transgender woman, mid 30s

PERSON 5: Male, mid 20s

PROLOGUE

The audience is split into two sections, facing each other.

In the space between them, 'the stage', are two chairs facing each other, with their sides perpendicular to the audience. A and T are seated in these chairs. A is checking his phone, T is reviewing files. At the far end of the room, behind A, is a projection screen.

Scattered at random within the audience, are Persons 1, 2, 3, 4 and 5. Ideally, two of these individuals are seated on one side of the room, and three of them are seated on the other.

We hear a recorded voice. This recording will have been conducted by the actor playing Person 2.

VOICE. Your lordships, I stand before you in the matter of *Navtej Singh Johar v. Union of India*. Five years ago, this court made a decision that impacted the lives of millions of LGBTQ persons in this country. A decision that said LGBTQ persons were minuscule minorities, undeserving of their so-called rights. A decision that has been publicly acknowledged by this very court as a 'discordant note' within its institutional history of protecting rights.

Your lordships, once again, we argue that Section 377 of the Indian Penal Code is unconstitutional. Our petitioners stand in this courtroom before you and ask you a question: How strongly must we love, knowing we are unconvicted felons? How long do we have to wait?

We have waited. We have waited a hundred and fifty eight years. We have waited and watched as our fundamental freedoms have remained restrained under a colonial-era law, forcing us to live as second-class citizens.

And so, your lordships.

In the matter of millions of LGBTQ citizens in this country who have waited. In the matter of my clients who have lived their lives in the shadow of a law, waiting.

We ask: On what side of history will this Court stand?

A pause.

We hear the opening bars of The Beatles' 'All You Need Is Love' as a flurry of images begin to play on the screen. All the images are responses to the Supreme Court of India's Navtej Singh Johar v. Union of India *decision: newspaper clippings, public demonstrations, marches, rebranded corporate logos, all celebrating the decriminalization of same-sex intimacy in the country. The music fades.*

PERSON 2 (*stands up*). The great German thinker, Johann Wolfgang von Goethe, had said, 'I am what I am, so take me as I am.' The emphasis on the unique being of an individual is the salt of their life. Denial of self-expression is inviting death.

(*A beat*) Justice Dipak Misra, *Navtej Singh Johar v. Union of India*

Person 2 sits down.

PERSON 3 (*stands up, reads from the stack*). 'The love that dare not speak its name' is how the love that exists between same-sex couples was described by Lord Alfred Douglas, the lover of

Oscar Wilde, in his poem 'Two Loves' published in 1894 in Victorian England.

(*A beat*) Justice Rohinton Nariman, *Navtej Singh Johar v. Union of India.*

Person 3 sits down.

PERSON 4 (*stands up*). Statutes like Section 377 give people ammunition to say 'this is what a man is' by giving them a law which says 'this is what a man is not'.

(*A beat*) Justice D. Y. Chandrachud, *Navtej Singh Johar v. Union of India.*

Person 4 sits down.

PERSON 5 (*stands up*). LGBT persons deserve to live a life unshackled from the shadow of being 'unapprehended felons'.

(*A beat*) Justice Indu Malhotra, *Navtej Singh Johar v. Union of India.*

Person 5 sits down.

PERSON 4 (*stands up*). The fundamental rights chapter is like the North Star in the universe of constitutionalism in India. Constitutional morality always trumps any imposition of a particular view of social morality by majoritarian regimes.

(*A beat*) Justice Nariman.

Person 4 sits down.

PERSON 5 (*stands up*). It is difficult to right the wrongs of history. But we can certainly set the course for the future. That we can do by saying that LGBT persons have a constitutional right to equal citizenship in all its manifestations.

(*A beat*) Justice Chandrachud.

Person 5 sits down.

PERSON 2 (*stands up*). History owes an apology to the members of this community and their families for the delay in providing redressal for the ignominy and ostracism that they have suffered through the centuries.

(*A beat*) Justice Malhotra.

Person 2 sits down.

PERSON 3 (*stands up*). Sexual orientation is an essential and innate facet of privacy. The right to privacy takes within its sweep the right of every individual to express their choices in terms of sexual inclination without the fear of persecution.

(*A beat*) Justice Mishra.

Person 3 sits down.

PERSON 2 (*stands*). Section 377 of the Indian Penal Code—

PERSON 3 (*stands*). —insofar as it criminalizes—

PERSON 4 (*stands*). —consensual sexual conduct—

PERSON 5 (*stands*). —between adults of the same sex—

PERSON 4. 'cannot be regarded as constitutional'

PERSON 3: 'is unconstitutional'

PERSON 2. 'is unconstitutional'

PERSON 5. 'is violative of Articles 14, 15, 19 and 21 of the Constitution.'

All of them sit back down.

THERAPY I

A. So it's like you're seated in the plane, buckled in.

T. All right.

A. And the pilot's done with their announcements and the flight attendants have finished that dance routine you never see but you really should.

T. Correct.

A. And then the plane starts to taxi on the runway, and it's slowly gathering speed, and then it's gathering more speed, till that roaring sound begins, and then if you think oh maybe this is when I want to get off, maybe this is one of those flights that's going to be a statistic in the papers, but then you can't really, there's no way you can stop the flight, theoretically you could fake a heart attack maybe and then they'd ground the plane but you're not going to fake a heart attack, so you're just there strapped in and then hoping that this isn't going to become a statistic and there is nothing you can do to stop this plane from taking off.

T. All right.

A. So yeah, that's what I think this is like—

T. You think love is like being on a plane taxiing on the runway—

A. No, not love, love—

T. Sorry, falling in love—

A. No, trying to stop yourself from falling in love.

43

T. Yes, thank you, got it. So (*consults her notes*) 'in terms of panic levels and futility, resisting the inexorable tug of falling in love is roughly equivalent to halting a speeding plane about to take off on the runway.'

A. Couldn't have put it better myself.

T. I'm quoting your Twitter feed—

A. Jokes!

(*Therapist is unresponsive*)

I mean I thought that was funny—

T. No, no, it was definitely funny, it was a good joke.

A. Thank you.

T. So you like approval?

A. Who doesn't?

T. Do you crave it?

A. Everybody on social media—

T. I'm not on social media—

A. Well many, many people are and nobody puts up a message, a tweet, a picture without the hope of it receiving approval.

T. Sure, but I'm not talking about the many other people—

A. OK yes, yes, of course, I like approval but what does that have to do with falling in love?

T. Maybe nothing,

A. So how do we fix me?

T. You're not broken,

A. Because I'm a legal citizen now,

T. You said illegality didn't affect you?

A. How did you—

T. Facebook.

A. There's just no privacy—

T. As your therapist—

A. You know, doctor—

T. Therapist—

A. Therapist—

T. You can use my name.

A. Tarini, that idea was said in a certain context, and yes, OK, while there is possibly a huge emotional cost to being an unapprehended felon, I personally was fine and unaffected—disaffected? No, unaffected—when we had the law. I mean I'm very happy that the Uber map shows you a little rainbow now, it appeals to me aesthetically and I'm celebrating with everyone, but yes, illegality wasn't such a burden.

T. So what brings you here?

A. I was born in—

T. We don't have to go into your childhood.

A. So we're not going to talk about my daddy issues?

T. When they're relevant.

A. Because I definitely have daddy issues.

T. Who doesn't?

(*A beat*)

Jokes! So where do you want to start?

A. OK, I think 2012 is a good place to start. I am in love, it always starts with love, with me, but this one is big. I'm with capital *l* LOVE with this guy. I thought I knew what love was, I'd dated other men, I'd been in proper relationships and they'd ended and I'd cried and I thought I knew love.

T. And then you meet this new person?

A. Not new though. I first saw him in my second year in law school—he'd come to do a lecture, he was speaking about queer rights and it wasn't one of those love-at-first-sight things, I mean that's not really a thing anyway, but this was—you want to know how it was different?

T. If you want to tell me.

A. Well I think it might be relevant.

T. Everything you say is relevant.

A. OK. He was different. It was different. We'd known each other for years, we'd stayed in touch, I finished law school, we began working in the same space, and I was seeing someone, and then this thing happened.

T. You were with someone else?

A. Irrelevant now. In the grand scheme of things.

T. OK. So . . . this thing happened?

A. We started reading. We read the Greeks. The ancient Greeks. Greek literature. I don't know how it began exactly, but we would just work our way through these texts, he'd mail me an essay about the philosophy of Plato and I'd share with him a fragment of Sappho and then we both read the Symposium together.

T. You sat and read the book together.

A. No not physically together, and anyway I read ebooks and he's a physical person—like he physically reads books, though he's also like really physically buff I suppose, but no, about books he's all about the paper—I should probably mention he was about ten–fifteen years older than me—

T. Ten or fifteen?

A. —Sixteen, he was sixteen years older than me—and we're reading *The Symposium*, and it's about these eight men talking about love and one of the subplots, I guess, is this older guy Socrates, you know, *The* Socrates is being pursued, frantically pursued by this young, strapping lad, Alcibiades. And Socrates plays this game where he's kind of teasing Alcibiades and dazzling him with words and wisdom but also not really going there. And one day I realized we were basically Socrates and Alcibiades.

T. Feel free to elaborate . . .

A. As in, you know, he was the older wise man and I was the young ingénue thirsting for wisdom, and generally thirsty, and we were in this little dance where we'd throw words and ideas from the Greeks at each other every day, but nothing happened until this one night when everything came together.

T. And what happened this night?

A. We came together.

(*Therapist remains impassive and merely nods.*)

OK, tough crowd. And actually there was no simultaneity in our coming, I'm pretty sure he didn't actually, but we will put a pin in that—so, OK, we were at this restaurant, a bunch of us getting drunk and talking about love and he was there and I remember we were giving each other these little knowing glances when the conversation moved to eros—erotic love— and at some point in the evening, the two of us, Socrates and I, were alone in an elevator, the others had gone ahead, and we kissed, finally, we kissed and it was the most incredible thing, it was perfect.

T. And then?

A. Well then we obviously had sex. Really good sex. Except for the part where I'm not sure if he came—

T. What happened with this Socrates person generally?

A. We got into a relationship, at some point.

T. Past tense?

A. And at some point, we got out. He got out. It took me a bit longer.

T. You mean he moved on before you did?

A. I mean he dumped me, after months of not wanting to be with me, and then it took me about two years to really let go.

T. Have you let go?

A. Oh I've dated other people after that—

T. But have you let go?

A. We're friends, and I'm happy, and he's with someone else now.

T. Have you let go?

A. I have no desire to be with him.

T. Have you let go?

A. What does that mean?

T. Good. That's a start.

PERSON 1. 2001. That is when it began.

This is a case about patience. Perseverance. We have been doing this for two decades. Longer, actually, but if you want to be official about history then, yes, we filed the petition in December 2001. Nobody was talking about this issue, nobody knew what the petition was about, the media was not on our side.

But we filed it. Not everyone was happy with us, they said we had jumped the gun, they asked what would happen if we lost. They said why bring attention to a law that is barely being used?

But the law was being used. That year the police had conducted raids on an NGO in Lucknow—an NGO that was working on HIV/AIDS—and arrested some of its staff for abetting the crime under Section 377. That's how easy it was for the law to get a hold of you.

So that year we filed a petition before the Delhi High Court. And then, two years later, the court took notice, only to dismiss us—377 is an academic issue, they said. An academic issue, nobody is affected by this law.

Did we give up? No. We took to the streets. We marched and rallied, we spoke up, more people joined the case, more groups came together. It was a marathon, and we ran it tirelessly, and then in 2009 we won. And we could breathe as a community, as lawyers, as activists, as civil society, we could breathe for a while, but only for a while because then an astrologer decided to file an appeal before the Supreme Court. Suresh Kumar Koushal didn't have anything to do with the case, but the Court decided to take up the appeal anyway.

We thought we were safe, but to be sure, we worked at getting more briefs before the court. Parents of LGBT persons, mental-health practitioners, teachers, a member of parliament, all these groups came together before the court. But the court didn't hear us then. They called us a minuscule minority, they said we didn't deserve our so-called rights. But we didn't give up, we continued to fight, we took the fight back to the court. People are talking about it as if the case began only in the last two years. Some five rich celebrities wake up one day and decide to file their own case and suddenly that's the only story.

PERSON 2. We're not saying we initiated the case, we're saying we brought the new strategy—

PERSON 1. It's not your turn, you'll get your chance—

PERSON 2. Like you got your chance for twenty years?

PERSON 1. Exactly my point: we fought for twenty years—more than that. This is an almost three-decade-long fight. This is a story about perseverance.

THERAPY II

A. If I go right back to the beginning, sure. I think I can remember a time when I wasn't anxious. If I try hard, I think, it's there, it's there in the moments when I'm ten? There are extended periods of time where I didn't feel these spikes . . . this little lead ball lodged in my gut . . . or my skull shrinking into my brain and this pounding in my ears . . . I know there was a time I didn't have any of that.

T. And when does it flare up?

A. When doesn't it flare up?—Everything is a trigger—the metro coming late, traffic stopping, the buzz of my phone, the move—

T. No, do you recall a time when it began to noticeably flare up?

A. I remember dreading this thing we used to have in law school—the Socratic method—you call on a student at random and you start interrogating them—they call it a great pedagogic tool, it's like how Socrates would call on his disciples . . .

T. So you were put on the spot?

A. We all were—and it was so exciting and challenging at first—this rush of adrenalin, everyone watching you, and then this surge of excitement if you've got it right . . .

T. And when you got it wrong?

A. It could be humiliating, but we just tried harder.

T. So you were taught to look forward to this sense of dread and positive release?

A. It felt like the best way to learn how to be a lawyer, how else do you learn?

T. I don't know, I trained to be a therapist.

A. And I'm so thankful for your training.

T. Was there anything else in law school that you found challenging?

A. In terms of my anxiety?

T. Yes.

A. Coming out was challenging. That took a few years, start to finish, pretty anxiety inducing. And then the whole 377 thing.

T. I thought you said it didn't make a difference to your life?

A. Yeah not in terms of—I didn't ever think the police would just pick me up someday on account of doing sex things with men or whatever—it's just—I only learnt I was gay at the time I realized it was a criminal offence to be gay and—well, that's not the most relaxing experience.

T. And your former partner, you called him Socrates . . .

A. Yeah but that has nothing to do with this . . .

T. Didn't you say he was a mentor figure for you?

A. He was older, and we bonded over literature, yes—I called it a literary seduction.

T. What did he call it?

A. Sex. He wasn't super-creative.

T. Do you think it meant different things to the two of you?

A. Sure, at first. But then he sent me this poem. A poem about eros, by Sappho. And I remember opening the poem—he'd emailed it to me—and reading it, and I felt every sensation it was describing at that moment. Tongue breaking, thin fire racing under skin, the drumming that filled my ears, all of it.

T. So what did the poem mean for you?

A. Proof. That he felt the same way.

T. But is it possible that he just felt it was a beautiful poem and wanted to share it with someone he had an intellectual and physical connection with?

A. It was a beautiful poem.

T. But it was more than that for you.

A. It was more than that for us.

T. Is that what he said?

A. He mailed it to me. Without comment. Without prefix. That was all. What more did he need to say?

T. Did he make you feel anxious?

A. He made me feel like I finally knew love.

T. Was that an anxious sensation?

A. He was—he is—the love of my life. It was the best thing to ever happen to me. It made me feel things in a way I didn't know was possible. When we kissed in that elevator for the first time—you know that red is a colour, but you don't realize that it can also be a feeling, you don't think about how it can also be the air you breathe, the touch of somebody's skin . . .

T. That sounds a lot like anxiety . . .

A. Sure, maybe that's what it is, maybe love and anxiety are the same thing.

T. That sounds depressing.

A (*looks at the table between them*). Does anyone actually use those tissues?

T. Anxiety is something that our body learns.

A. Like do you know when they're about to break down and then do you hold them out?

T. I'm just asking you to—

A. What if I'm *this* close to breaking down and I'm asking about the tissues pre-emptively?

T. You're not close to breaking down.

PERSON 2. If you break it down, this is a case about strategy. The right strategy at the right moment. It's about knowing when a strategy is not working and when there's time for a change. The last time we stood before the Supreme Court in 2012, the judges asked a question: 'Do you know any gay people?' We couldn't answer. Such an easy question, and no one could speak up at that moment. There were no LGBTQ voices before the court.

PERSON 1. We had affidavits filed in the case. They were read before the court—

PERSON 2. What was your case called?

PERSON 1. *Naz Foundation v. Union of India.*

PERSON 2. Is that an individual's name?

PERSON 1. You know as well as I do that we still filed individual affidavits—

PERSON 2. I thought it was my turn to speak. Thanks. So. We went back to the drawing board. We asked: How do we get people's stories, people's voices before the court? And we got people, five brave men and women who were able to stand before the Court, and swear in a public document that they were gay, that they were lesbian, that they had lived a life in the shadow of the law. This case, the case that finally won, is called *Navtej Singh Johar v. Union of India*. It is signified by the name of an individual who told the court about his relationship with another man, a relationship that has spanned decades living under the shadow of a law—

PERSON 1. A law that hardly affected them—they were happily going about their lives in their fancy South Delhi houses—

PERSON 2. And where exactly do you live?

(*A beat*)

Anyway, that wasn't the only set of stories, we got another group of students to tell their stories to the court. We got some of them with us in the Supreme Court. We made the human cost of the case tangible. This case needed a story to win. We gave the court a story.

A. I've been doing the whole casual-dating thing.

T. Good! How often?

A. It can vary.

T. But if you had to try and—

A. Last week I scheduled three in the same day—I was doing this whole comparative analysis—

T. That's a lot of dates.

A. That's a lot of judgement.

T. Does dating like this make you feel happier?

A. It makes me feel more desired.

T. What about when someone doesn't reciprocate?

A. When I get rejected, I can always move on to the next one—that's the beauty of it. I go home, I open the app, and there's always going to be someone else.

T. And what are you looking for in these men?

A. I like it if they read. I hate it when they use the word sapiosexual, that makes my skin crawl. I like it if it looks like they take care of themselves. I like it if they really like what they're doing.

T. Are these things you take from him?

A. From—

T. Socrates.

A. I know what you're thinking—

T. Tell me what you're thinking.

A. I'm trying my best to not compare. Obviously, I know that's not fair to these guys, or to myself.

T. Do you still find yourself doing it?

A. Never consciously—I know that he was a one-time thing so that can't happen again—

T. So how does it happen?

A. OK, so the guy will make a literary reference, and then I'll get excited and ask more and it'll turn out that it's somehow superficial, like, we all know the phrase 'Call me Ishamel' right, that's not a special thing by itself . . .

T. So you're disappointed that these men haven't read *Moby Dick*?

A. When Socrates referred to stories and ideas, there was a sense that he'd internalized them, it was coming from a space where he'd made the stories a part of himself. On these dates, it's just banter.

T. Sounds like a high bar.

A. But I'm allowing people to clear it.

T. A great service to humanity.

A. Are you allowed to be this mean?

T. Sorry, did you say you were lowering your standards?

A. Changing them. I get that, it's never quite going to be the same, so I'm trying to look for other things. Like, six months after we broke up, I met this activist guy at a conference and we had a connection. Turns out he lived in a different country, so there were geographic limitations there, but I gave it a shot, and it was fun, for a while. He was closer to my age, he was a great cook, wasn't much of a reader, not in the same way, but there were other things that worked.

T. What stopped working?

A. Long distance, like I just said.

T. But you've worked around that before.

A. Right. OK, yes, I have.

T. So what was it?

A. It was a small thing.

T. It's always the small things.

A. So . . . he was a really private person. And he didn't want for us to share, for me to share the relationship with the larger world—and the breaking point happened around then.

T. Was he closeted?

A. No, I said, he's an activist, a queer-rights activist.

T. So he's just a private person.

A. Yeah, that's what he said.

T. What did you hear?

A. The sound of him saying it . . .

T. How did you understand what he said?

A. That he didn't want to be too public about this.

T. Yes, but what did that actually mean to you? What was your specific emotional response?

A. It was . . . I felt slighted?

T. That was it?

A. No, more, I felt . . . humiliated

T. Even though he said it was about his issues?

A. Yeah, but if I was good enough, he wouldn't have wanted this to be a secret.

T. So he never introduced you to his friends?

A. Well, OK, that's not—he did—

T. So maybe it wasn't about you being good enough then?

A. Yeah, we did meet a bunch of people as a 'couple' or whatever . . .

T. But then he told you he didn't want you to be too public about it?

A. Yes.

T. And that triggered something strong enough for you to end things?

A. Yes. I just have a sense of self-esteem, and what he did, what he asked me to do—not do—that felt wrong.

T. I could argue that a healthy ego would perhaps also be able to discern the difference between a person wanting privacy and a person being embarrassed of you.

A. I do have a healthy self-esteem.

T. You do. But something about this completely dislodged your sense of self. Who did you become?

PERSON 3. This case is about how things can change.

For me, it's a case about my parents.

I came out to them six years ago, the week before the hearings in *Suresh Kumar Koushal* began. They were angry, they were sad, they were confused, all of these things. When they took me to a psychiatrist, he told us that my homosexuality was a mental disorder, possibly the result of a tumour in my hypothalamus, which he could cure with aggressive instant treatment. When I pointed out the World Health Organization's clear position on homosexuality not being a disease and threatened to file a complaint against him, he tried to convince my parents I was suffering from a form of schizophrenia.

I stormed out of the doctor's office. I almost stormed out of my parents' lives. Something broke between us that day, and even on the few occasions we spoke, it was always by talking around the issue. My mother and I still made some progress, and Bollywood helped us—every time a movie with a queer character was released, we could talk about that as some kind of proxy. My father, on the other hand, was consistent in his silence around this issue.

When the *Suresh Kumar Koushal* decision came out in 2013, I was studying in the US. It was a particularly snowy winter that year, they were calling it the year of the polar vortex. My father called that day, a few hours after the decision was announced. He asked how I was dealing with the cold, he asked whether I was taking adequate precautions to keep myself warm. We spoke politely about the weather for two minutes. There was a pause in the conversation, maybe three seconds, it could have been the line dropping but I let myself think it was because he wanted to say one more thing and couldn't bring himself to. The conversation ended there, anyway.

And then something changed. I'd been so wrapped up in my journey, I didn't really have a chance to think about the paths he'd been travelling. I don't know what journey he took to get there, but something changed. On the 9th of July 2018, the Supreme Court began hearing its final arguments in the *Navtej Johar* petition. I saw a missed call from him that morning, and then every morning for the next three days. I was too busy watching the hearings to take the call, but if I'm honest, I was also dreading what he would say, how I would respond.

He called on the fourth morning again, and this time I answered. His voice shook—my father, the most confident, assertive man I know, this man who at one point managed a staff of hundreds, his voice shook, his voice shook as he asked me if I would like him and my mother to come to the court, if that would help, if I might need their support at this time?

It took me a while to find my voice.

Things can change.

THERAPY IV

A. It's different this time. You can't script these things, you know.

T. Don't you do that with your work?

A. I mean, you can't plan them in advance, right? What are the chances? What are the odds that—here's the scene, I'm in the audience, watching a play, in London, the first play that I have written, and somehow it's made its way to London, and next to me is this man, this stranger, he's cute, I've checked him out in the hallway, and he gets the seat next to me. And when the play starts, they do a little shout-out to the playwright, like hey there's our guy, there's our lawyer who happens to write plays, and I wave, and this man, this stranger, he just leans in and he says—

PERSON 3. Oh so now I'll have to say it's brilliant.

A. And I say, Well, only if you want me to kiss you afterwards. And he says—

PERSON 3. Depends on how well you write.

A. And then for the next hour, we watch the play without acknowledging each other, and it finishes, and he turns towards me and says—

PERSON 3. Well, that was pretty fucking brilliant, wasn't it?

A. And I ask, Are you telling me this because you want to make out with me or because you were into the play, to which he replies—

PERSON 3. Why don't I give you the full review, while we're making out?

A. BOOM. Just like that. I could not have scripted it better.

T. And you kissed?

A. Well, we had this little Q-and-A thing afterwards, but then he caught me at the bar and we went out for a smoke, and then we kissed.

T. I thought you don't smoke?

A. Yeah, no, he does.

T. How do you feel about that?

A. I mean it's not ideal.

T. Didn't you tell me once you felt smokers didn't respect their bodies?

A. I feel like I'm being cross-examined.

T. Just going back to what you've said in the past.

A. Literally how cross-examination works.

T. Yes, and you said—

A. OK, so my ideal partner wouldn't smoke, but then can we get back to the story about this more-than-ideal partner?

T. He's your partner now?

A. Well, you and I haven't had a session in two months.

T. When did you meet him?

A (mumbles). Three weeks.

T. Sorry?

A. It's been three weeks, all right? It moved quick!

T. OK, so you had the play and then you kissed and—

A. And we kissed again on the Tube and we explored the city, we met his friends and they're great, it's a little coterie of artists and musicians—oh he's a music composer, I didn't mention that, and then we went for this concert, and we kissed in parks and then I'm at the airport just walking to the check-in counter, and he texts just as I'm walking to the counter, again you can't script these things right, and he says—

PERSON 3. That was just not enough time.

A. And I say, Yes, yes, it wasn't enough time, would you like some more time? And then he says—

PERSON 3. I would do anything for a time-turner.

A. Which is a Harry Potter reference, so you know if I'm not already swooning, and so I go to the ticketing counter and I ask for a rebooking two days later. And I call him and I say, Mischief managed, which is—

T. A Harry Potter reference, yes—

A. And I can tell he's just leapt out of the bed in excitement, and so we got two more days of kissing and walking and doing sex things and it was amazing and now, yes, we are together.

T. How are you feeling?

A. I feel like I'm high. I feel like I'm walking around with this cushion of warmth hugging me, I feel like this is right, just all of it, it's . . . this is what I've been looking for.

T. What about the smoking?

A. What about it? That's a tiny detail—are you hearing this story?

T. You feel good.

A. I feel like something . . . is healing. Something inside me is whole, and fixed. That ball of anxiety that I carry around all the time. It's gone. So I guess I feel complete. This is it. I'm taking a break, spending the summer with him. And I just know . . . it's going to be different this time.

PERSON 4. Nothing's going to change. Anyway, 377 was never such a big issue for us, no?

I remember they first punished me for wearing girls' clothes when I was six. I was a very naughty child, and I would keep stealing clothes from my sister, and then when they caught me they would say you write in a book 500 times 'I must not wear girls' clothes,' even then I didn't think I was doing it purposefully or anything, but I wrote 'I must wear girls' clothes'— they really got fed up with me, you know? And then I saw a hijra woman for the first time when I was with my mother shopping on the road, I was ten and I looked at the hijra woman, and I wanted to go to her, and my mother suddenly grabbed my hand and said, 'Be careful of them, they will take you away.' But I wanted them to take me away.

Soon I became good at attempting suicide. Don't look like that—obviously, I'm here now, and anyway, my point is that I was good at attempting, bad at actually doing it. I was terrible, OK? I had no sense. It was funny how bad I was.

The first time—I was a very well-fed child, OK? I must have been twelve and I had seen enough Bollywood films in which they hang from the fan, so then one day I decided, OK, enough time to try this, and I managed to reach the fan, picked a very nice yellow dupatta, obviously it had to look good, and then— *dhad!*—the fan only came down, it couldn't support my weight.

Then next time I thought, OK, let's try the other big Bollywood style—wrist cutting. But—you are supposed to cut your hand like *this* if you want to die, not like *this*, how would I know, I am not a science student—I only got enough marks to get into arts—so I made a bad cut, and it was not bleeding properly, just paining a lot, so then I just had to go to the hospital and get stitches for nothing.

Third time was the most embarrassing. I really like the Juhu Chowpatty—I was born and brought up in Bombay, I thought, *theek hai*, this is a good location. But then I started walking into the sea, and the sand gets really slippery, no? So you get scared, and then there is all this plastic, it's not very clean, and then that water is also so salty, so when it goes into your mouth, it's really yuck. I started screaming at this point and some men on the beach came out to save me. They thought they were saving a woman. I think they were disappointed when we got back to the beach. But they didn't abuse me, so that was good.

And then I thought, *chalo*, three times it hasn't happened, try something else now, try to live. And then there was this law—377—there was some activism to do—*kaun sa kanoon sabse battar bol bol ke thak gaye**—there were NGOs coming up—that was one way for me to be employed. I had to do a little bit of sex work in the start, but now we are getting more funding so it's fine for me.

* We were tired of chanting 'which is the worst law?'

Now this law is gone, *theek hai,* we'll do other work. Our NGO will still get money. All these other new issues coming up, and the old ones haven't gone away, anyway.

PERSON 3. So do you feel like nothing changed at all?

PERSON 4. I took an Uber to go to work the day after the decision. The route map was a rainbow. That was new. Then I got off the Uber and the men on the road outside my office started calling me names, and I clapped my hands at them. Same thing they've done for the last three years, same thing I've done for the last three years. What can this Supreme Court do for me?

THERAPY V

A. I think it was the smoking that really killed it. I also felt suffocated. I felt trapped. But I think it was the smoking.

(*T nods*)

You're not going to say I told you so?

T. I'm going to say I may have asked you about the possibility of you perhaps too easily letting what you have described to me as a 'deal-breaker' temporarily not function as a 'deal-breaker' and maybe—

A. God, you really should be a lawyer.

(*A long pause*)

You know, I sleep badly. It's been this way for years, I fall asleep, and it's fine, and then I wake at 5 a.m. and it's like there is a lead band around my heart, and nothing will make it go away. But with him, it went away. I remember we'd sleep like babies, I would be drowsy, I would wake up to the sun, and he'd still be fast asleep and I would feel so much peace. And I remember telling him, this is a chemical reaction, there's oxytocin flooding through my body and you're causing it.

And then one night, I came back late, he was drunk. He was drunk and he was being silly, and it was the most innocent of things, he wanted me to dance with him, and I was exhausted but I did it and I remember this stab of resentment, and then he kissed me and his mouth tasted of ash, I could taste on his lips the dozen cigarettes he'd probably smoked that day, and I felt the resentment multiplying exponentially, and then he sleepily asked me about sex and I said sure, we'd get to it, and then the next morning came.

And the next morning, I was up at 5 a.m. It was back— the anxiety, the lead bands, they were there and they were screaming at me louder than ever and now they were saying, Look, there's a new cause. There's a new root for your malaise. And it's sleeping right beside you.

T pushes the box of tissues towards A. A glares at her.

T. When did you tell him?

A. I waited a few days. I thought maybe it would go away. Or that the other thing would come back. The high. I kept willing for it to come back.

T. But it didn't.

A. How does it work? How can it just come and go without warning? How is this not the most terrifying thing in the world, how can I wake up one morning and realize I'm out of love with this man who is otherwise perfect for me? How could Socrates wake up one morning and realize he's out of love with me?

T. Maybe he wasn't perfect for you.

A. Maybe.

T. And you know that you weren't perfect for Socrates.

A. Possibly.

T. And then there's the other thing.

A. That I'm terrible at this stuff?

T. That nobody is actually perfect for anybody else. It's never not work. Sometimes you choose to do the work. Sometimes you decide it isn't worth the work. You can't choose how you feel, you can't choose when it comes and when it goes. But that other part—that you can choose.

PERSON 5. So I was like, hey, so wanna get married, and he goes, mmm, that's not how it works, and then I said, does that mean you don't love me, and then he says, no I mean there's no connection between marriage and love—ugh I know, right?—but also we can't actually get married, and then I said, well I thought you were a lawyer, didn't the court just say the Constitution has been changed or something and we can all be free, and then he just said, he had to leave the room for a bit, he was like, I just can't be with you right now, and this is the problem with dating lawyers, they get so technical about everything, I mean isn't the point now that everything is like—fair game?

PERSON 3. Excuse me, I'm sorry but—

PERSON 5. Exactly and then they keep trying to interrupt you or argue with you, always arguing. I mean, I don't even know if I want to get married, you know? Like maybe we could just buy a house together—maybe we could get a dog—maybe I can stop calling his mother Auntie and be like Mom!—I don't know—but something has to change, right?

PERSON 4. I understand, but—

PERSON 5. No, it's not fine! I mean look, when the judgement came out I was waiting on that little lawn outside the court . . . you remember, Delhi in early September, sticky bloody hot, but I thought good only, there were so many press people, good photo op, and then he came out of the court and it was so hard to get him to pose for a kiss—everybody was kissing, it was so sweet, and I said, look, maybe the top-tier gays will end up on the *Hindu* or the *Express* cover, sure, but maybe we can get on one of those online portals—

PERSON 2. Do you even know what this meeting is about?

PERSON 5. I thought we were just sharing feelings?

THERAPY VI

A. I'm trapped. I'm trapped with myself. I'm fundamentally incapable of change.

T. What did we say about expressing absolutes?

A. I *feel* like I'm trapped with myself and fundamentally incapable of change?

T. Never mind. You were telling me about your mother?

A. Right, my mother. She—she yelled at me yesterday.

T. I'm sorry to hear that.

A. No, it was—it wasn't bad yelling, she's just a bit exasperated—I told you, right? I've been doing this thing where I've been telling her about the new guy, and my love life. She said she wanted to know, and my friends are bored of hearing about it— you're probably bored of hearing about it.

T. You pay me to hear about your love life.

A. So you *are* bored hearing about it?

T. No, these stories are enthralling.

A. OK, so my mother, after I tell her about this new guy, she says, oh god knows what to do with this *Manmarziyaan* generation

T. What's the *Manmarziyaan* generation?

A. You know—from the movie?

(*T shakes head*)

Oh it's so good—OK, so—may I?—So, Taapsee Pannu is our protagonist and she's this feisty woman who knows what she wants and she wants Vicky Kaushal, because who doesn't, and he wants her, until the point where it comes to the possibility of marriage, and then he's confused—he still wants to be with her, he's just not sure about marriage—and then in comes Abhishek Bachchan who wants her and marriage and is totally chill about the fact that she's madly in love with Vicky because he's so calmly confident that she will come to love him, and he's not crazy because it actually starts happening and she's kind of in love with two people—

T. Sorry, but where does the new guy come into the picture?

A. Abhishek Bachchan?

T. No, the new man in your life, the one you were telling your mother about.

A. Right, OK, so he's—he was—is—I don't know what he is now, but he was till recently an acquaintance who happens to be in a five-year monogamous relationship with another man, and we now know that I am really wise and enlightened about these things so of course I wasn't going to do anything about it, even though I thought he was really attractive, I was going to let this go . . .

T. But . . .

A. But we went for a movie, *this* movie actually, and then—so he's seated to my right and we're watching the movie—

T. What movie?

A. *Manmarziyaan!* Obviously, that's how the *Manmarziyaan-*generation thing—God, Tarini, you have to keep up—anyway, so we're watching this movie, and imagine this is the armrest, and there's his hand, his bare uncovered forearm and there's my hand, also uncovered, and they're just placed next to each other, and at one point they brush, and neither of us removes their hands. He definitely wasn't budging a millimetre and at first I think, oh, it's this white-boy confidence—he's white—and I think it's nothing, but then we're half an hour into the movie, and we just haven't budged from this position, and I'm looking out from the corner of my eye and I see his other arm is comfortably nestled in his lap, and so I decide to a little experiment. When the movie breaks for intermission, we leave our seats, we walk out, and when we walk back in I just switch seats with him, make some silly excuse. And now I'm waiting to see where he puts his arm. I place mine very confidently on this side of the armrest. And then he puts his arm on my side. And by the end of the movie our forearms are almost fused together, a bit sweaty from the sustained contact actually, and so I turn around and ask him up front—did I just imagine that or is there a thing that just happened here?

PERSON 3. No, that was not in your head.

A. And then a pause.

PERSON 3. I'm drawn to you.

T. And that's when you fell in love?

A. No, of course not, it's not that easy.

(*A beat*)

OK, it took a week. But at that point he told me that he was drawn to me, that he was unsure of where his relationship was going, that it felt like we had some sort of connection. And I thought it was nothing, I thought this is child's play, he was only around in the country for two weeks anyway, so I said, It's fine, we'll ignore this, you focus on your monogamy, and we'll put a pin on this sudden conflagration of chemistry, and you've said you want to explore the monuments of Delhi so we will proceed as planned.

(*A beat*)

And then, yes, somewhere between Begumpur Masjid and Sanjayvan, I fell in love with him.

T. And you told him this?

A. Not in so many words, but he knew. But he's a good person who's committed to his partner.

T. Which is why he walks through deserted Delhi parks with men he's clearly attracted to?

A. Nothing happened!

(*A long pause*)

We held hands in a cab?

(*Another pause*)

We hugged?

(*Yet another pause*)

We had a long, lingering embrace the night before he left the country. I could feel all of him pressed up against me, my face buried in his neck, his hands dug into my hair, it was a long embrace. But that's all. Nothing else, no carnal intercourse against the order of nature, or within the order of nature. Not even a kiss.

T. So he's gone?

A. Yes.

T. And you're still thinking about him?

A. It's been a month, and I think about him every day.

T. So what do you like about Mr *Manmarziyaan?*

A. Can we call him Mr Taapsee? I feel like that tracks better.

T. What do you like about Mr Taapsee?

A. He's kind. Kind in a way that I don't think I am, and I liked that because it made me think that I could be more like that, if we were together. And he's warm and he's generous with his praise, I don't know how to put it better—and, he didn't keep secrets, not from me about where he was in his relationship, not with his partner about what he'd experienced with me, he was never less than completely honest.

T. What else?

A. He's awkward but in a way that's endearing, he always lets me finish my sentences, he's secure in his intelligence but he doesn't flaunt it . . . he has brown hair, well, that's not a plus or minus, that's a neutral thing . . . he likes the Beatles . . . he's my age . . . there are things that I think I can teach him, there are things that I think I can learn from him, I think we fit . . . I think we fit. And that makes no sense to me, because he is good and kind, so how do we fit? But we do.

T. You've mentioned this point about kindness twice. Do you think you're unkind?

A. I don't think I'm Mother Teresa.

T. You're a human-rights lawyer?

A. Oh, that is not a standard for goodness, trust me.

T. Are you good to your friends?

A. I don't think I'm a bad friend but—I've done things.

T. What have you done?

A. When I was in the fifth grade—

T. You're basing your moral worth on your ten-year-old self?

A. I know all kids do stupid things, but I wasn't like the other kids, I would get punished for running to the library because I was so scared of the sports lessons, I'd get laughed at for presenting poems on our talent-sharing day, and I dealt with it all right, I knew I was different but it was fine, there were always books to take comfort in, or places to escape to, and I was OK. But then, one day this other kid joined the school. He was more clearly effeminate than I was and he joined our class, and maybe if I was someone else, I would have seen in him a friend, an ally, some kind of kinship. Instead I saw a scapegoat, I saw someone who could take my place in the food chain. The week he joined I led the brigade in teasing him, bullying him mercilessly, and it was such a relief to be in a position of power. I remember this one time the entire class made fun of his lisp and I stood right in front. I remember the specific hurt in his eyes reserved for me who should have done better and should have understood.

And now, I meet a man who would never hurt a thing or a person on purpose, I think he'd apologize to a bush if he walked into it. And for a second it looked like he saw something good in me. And then it was gone.

T. And where do things stand now?

A. Gone. He called it off before we even had a chance, before it really began. And it makes sense, I see why he did that—he's with the right person already—so, spoiler alert, but Taapsee picks Abhishek Bachchan at the end because he is kind and reliable and can promise her a kind of stability, and that's what this guy has with his partner already. I was the fun Vicky Kaushal excitement but that's not the one people pick. Not the one Taapsee picks, anyway.

T. So it's over?

A. Except that it never really began? And I feel lost and I feel . . . I'm just frustrated, I feel like I just don't learn. I was once again in an impossible situation where I had no control, I just don't . . . I just don't learn. I just don't change. Things don't change with me.

T. Except—that they do.

A. I'm once again in an impossible romantic entanglement. What's changed?

T. We've had forty-five sessions. I've seen you for one year now.

A. Yes, I know, you're very expensive.

T. We've had forty-five hours of therapy. And this is the first session you haven't brought up Socrates.

INTERLUDE VI

PERSON 3 : We're not sharing feelings, we're supposed to be planning the Pride march. Or Pride month or whatever.

PERSON 4. Or we should be anyway.

PERSON 5. It didn't sound like you were doing much planning.

PERSON 1. We're deliberating on the theme.

PERSON 2. I've said it multiple times this case is about—

PERSON 1. You.

PERSON 2. Excuse me?

PERSON 1. It's about you. You've made it all about yourself. You've positioned yourself as the face of the case.

PERSON 2. I positioned the petitioners as the face of the case.

PERSON 1. It isn't your story to tell.

PERSON 2. Exactly, it's their story.

PERSON 1. Is that what you're saying in your media interviews?

PERSON 2. Oh, so you never had media interviews?

PERSON 1. That's not—

PERSON 2. Or is it just that yours had a lesser reach?

PERSON 1. We didn't want to make this a media circus.

PERSON 2. And maybe that was your mistake.

PERSON 1. At least we give collective acknowledgement.

PERSON 2. As long as you ensure it's you who gets to make the acknowledgement.

PERSON 1. We've been around from the start.

PERSON 2. And what did that get you?

PERSON 1. We won the case in the Delhi High Court in 2009.

PERSON 2. And you lost resoundingly in 2013.

PERSON 1. We all lost together! And we lost because of the judges.

PERSON 2. That wasn't the only reason.

PERSON 1. When you walked into the court this time in 2018, weren't the judges different?

PERSON 2. They were different because of the stories they'd been presented with.

PERSON 1. They were different because of the public advocacy and activism that had happened.

PERSON 4. The public advocacy and activism that we were doing on the ground.

PERSON 5. What, because we were sitting at home, is it?

PERSON 4. Actually, yes you were, and also you have homes.

PERSON 5. And your gharana isn't a house?

PERSON 4. I share a roof with eight people, where do you think I go to have sex?

PERSON 5. I mean, don't people pay you . . .

PERSON 4. You think the only sex I have is when people pay me?

PERSON 5. No, I'm just—

PERSON 4. Oh my god, this is the problem with you upper-caste gay fucking—

PERSON 5. How is caste relevant here?!

PERSON 4. What's your surname?

PERSON 5. That's not the point!

PERSON 3. I think the point is we're trying to figure out a central theme for Pride.

PERSON 1. About how we won the case—

PERSON 2. How *we* won the case—

PERSON 4. You lawyers are the problem, please, this god complex, whatever you did in the court, you did because of us—have you been to a single protest?

PERSON 1/PERSON 2 (*together*). We were busy in court!

PERSON 5. You don't talk, have you been to a single flash mob we've organized?

PERSON 4. You think flash mobs are the answer?

PERSON 5. We're creating queer visibility in spaces that count! Who comes to your protests?

PERSON 2. We gave the court a story it could use.

PERSON 1. Yes, and you happily wiped out this case's history.

FINAL THERAPY / INTERLUDE

A. I'm just not sure how me talking or not talking about Socrates is relevant to the larger point.

T. And what is the larger point?

A. I just shouldn't be dating anybody.

T. For?

A. For good. At all. I just need to step out of the game. It doesn't seem to work out for me or the others. It just doesn't work out. All of these stories, they just—I mean they're disasters, aren't they?

T. I've been reading the Greeks. *The Symposium*.

A. You read . . . Plato?

T. You keep going on about it.

A. You read Plato for *me*?

T. Do you know how much you pay me?

 (*A shrugs, acknowledging this point*)

 So you know the Aristophanes speech?

A. Do I know the Earth is round?

 (*A beat*)

 I'm sorry, please, go on.

T. So Aristophanes tells us about how long ago human beings existed in pairs—

A. Like, fused together, yes—

T. And they were happy and content roaming around in pairs all the time, so happy that they didn't need anything or anybody else, including the gods, so the gods decide to punish them—

A. Zeus sends down thunderbolts that rip apart all the pairs and they're scattered in different parts of the world—

T. And they're lonely and separated from the person they were meant to be with, and the only way they'll feel complete again is if they find the other person they were separated from.

A. They'll stop feeling pain and love will repair them.

T. It's a nice story. Do you believe it?

A. I mean . . . people believe that dead men get resurrected. People believe that prophets fly on horses. People believe that demonetization was a good idea.

T. What do you believe?

A. Obviously, I don't think there is some Big Bang Theory of the origin of love and I don't think we were all fused together in an early state of harmony.

T. And the rest of it?

A. I think that—I feel that it isn't the stupidest idea that there might be a person who gets what it is like, who understands you as well as you understand yourself, or maybe even better, and that when you meet and you connect, it's like everything falls into place.

T. Like the moment in the elevator with Socrates?

A. The elevator was real, that was a real moment.

T. So you found the person you were supposed to find, and then you lost them.

A. Or let them get away, yes.

T. Can you take me back to the elevator?

A. Aren't you exhausted with that story?

T. Can you walk me through it once more?

A. We get into an elevator. Sexy times happen. Years later I'm in therapy.

(*T crosses her arms and looks at him impassively.*)

Cool. Cool. All right. It's 2012. There's eight of us sitting on a rooftop, getting drunk talking about love.

T. Was it eight?

A. Yeah, like in *The Symposium*.

T. But are you sure it was eight?

A. Yes! I'm here. There's two people to my right. Then there's Socrates diagonally across. And then next to him, there's one, two people. So that's—

T. Seven.

A pause.

A. Right, right, OK, seven.

T. Do you think you remembered eight because that fit more neatly with the *Symposium* story?

A. It's a good story, but whatever, seven, eight, doesn't matter.

T. How many people could the elevator hold?

A. Six.

T. Was it pure chance that the two of you stayed upstairs?

A. He took a step forward. And I grabbed the back of his shirt. I held him back.

T. So you ensured that the two of you would get a ride in that elevator alone?

A. I influenced the odds.

T. And when you got inside, what happened?

A. That part doesn't change, we kissed.

T. What was going through your head?

A. That it was the most amazing kiss, that it was the most beautiful moment of my life, I had been in love with this man for years, and now—

T. What else was going through your head?

A. That we were both cheating on our boyfriends.

T. What else?

A. That my boyfriend was one of his closest friends.

T. How did that make you feel?

A. I told you, I'm not Martin Luther King.

T. You said Mother Teresa. Martin Luther King actually did have a string of extramarital affairs.

A. Uh—

T. But go on.

A. I know I should have been guilty, I know it should have felt wrong. For me, in that moment, all I could see, all I could think was—I was in love. I was in the moment that I thought I had waited for my entire life, I thought, this was it.

T. And what did he feel?

A. He—

T. Did he feel the same way?

PERSON 1. I thought it was exciting. I thought it was fun. It was great.

A. But that was all.

T. What did he say?

PERSON 1. We can't tell anyone. You can't tell anyone.

T. And what did you want?

A. I wanted to run through the streets and grab people and tell them that the most incredible thing had happened. I wanted to write the news in the skies, I was exploding with joy and I wanted the world to know. But he was ashamed.

PERSON 1. You tell anyone and this is over.

A. He was ashamed.

PERSON 1. It was wrong.

A turns towards Person 1.

A. Not wrong enough to end things with me. Not wrong enough to walk away from this. Just wrong enough to not tell the world.

PERSON 1. The world would have judged us.

A. So you decided to do all the judging yourself.

PERSON 1. It was good enough for you then.

A. It was. I thought it was all I deserved.

(*A turns back to therapist*)

I thought it was all I deserved. If I couldn't have all of his love, I'd settle for the little scraps he threw my way.

T. You like narratives. You like stories. All of us do, obviously. The only problem with a grand unifying narrative is that it can be incomplete.

PERSON 2. This is a case about bringing people's lives into the courtroom

PERSON 4. No, it's about how you've ignored our life stories.

PERSON 3. I think it's about how people can have conversations in spaces where it wasn't possible.

PERSON 5. No, it's about how we get to gay marriage!

PERSON 1. It's about honouring the decades of struggle that got us here.

T. You told yourself a story about this man. He dazzled you, he gave you something you'd never experienced before. So you told yourself he would heal something.

A. But what, because love is an illusion, that's impossible?

T. Not at all. I think love can be healing and reparative—I think it can do a lot. But I don't think this story and this man did any of that for you. I think it reinforced something else entirely. And I think you know what it was.

A. Should I be guessing?

T. I think you know the answer.

A. You know this is literally the Socratic method, right?

T. Seems to be your style?

A beat.

A. I felt . . . I felt . . . shame? That's what I felt. When he told me we had to keep things secret, I felt reduced, I felt ashamed, I felt smaller. And I didn't mind it, I didn't mind the shame, I didn't mind being told that my love was less or inferior.

T. And why do you think that was?

A. Because that's the story I've been telling myself for so long.

T. It's the shame you felt when you were bullying your classmate in school. It's the shame you felt when you found a word for who you were in law school.

A. The law didn't teach me to feel shame.

T. But it confirmed something you'd suspected for a while. It let you accept whatever twisted love was thrown at you.

A. Because I thought it's what I deserved. What I still deserve.

T. But that's not true.

A. Um, Mr Taapsee, hello.

T. Yes, exactly, Mr Taapsee.

A. That story does not end well!

T. That story involves you falling in love with a man who is kind and good and caring—

A. And unavailable.

T. Yes, and when you realized that was the case, you took a step back instead of pursuing him. But meanwhile, you felt love for a person who was genuinely good for you and who treated you with kindness and respect. That is not the same as chasing an illusion because it neatly fits a literary narrative. That's what you did with Socrates. It's not the same as settling for something because you don't think you deserve anything better. That's also what you did with Socrates. You like your ancient Greek stories, and that's fine. I don't think the Aristophanes story is nonsense. It's just incomplete.

A. You're telling me that in your professional-doctor opinion—

T. Therapist—

A. Therapist opinion, you're telling me that the concept of soulmates and finding your other half is not problematic?

T. I'm telling you that the people whom we love and who love us back can do wonderful things for us. I'm telling you love does have the potential to heal us or make us better or feel more whole or whatever you choose to call it. And I'm telling you that you just have to be careful about whom you're vulnerable to.

A. But this other half business—

T. Maybe we have multiple soulmates floating around the world. Maybe our soulmates are the friendships we build or the communities we foster. Sometimes, maybe our soulmates are also lovers. Whatever the case may be, every choice that you have made, every person you have allowed to enter your life, every person you've cared for and allowed yourself to be cared by— all of these made you healthier and more whole.

A. So I'm . . . OK?

T. You are so much more than OK. You spent years telling yourself a story about this man who was the love of your life and without whom you'd never be happy. And now you're finally letting go.

A. So I've been OK for a while?

T. Looks like it.

A. So basically, you're running a scam and overcharging me for no reason.

   (*A beat*)

A and T (*together*). Jokes!

Another beat.

A. But does this mean we're done?

T. I think so.

A. No more therapy?

T. Not until the next time you fuck up.

A. So next week then?

T. I think you'll be fine.

> *A swivels his chair around. Then turns right back. At this point, the other characters begin to get up and gradually start moving towards the stage, eventually forming a loose circle around A and T.*

PERSON 2. So we're done here?

PERSON 1. Nothing to say.

PERSON 4. OK.

PERSON 3. Wait. Guys, come on, it's Pride.

PERSON 5. You can't just keep repeating that!

PERSON 3. I meant, it's not just any Pride. It's the first Pride event we get to have after decriminalization. And yes, we can all disagree on what that means.

PERSON 5. That's what I'm saying, was it worth fighting for? Shouldn't we have focused on—

PERSON 3. Other issues, I agree . . .

PERSON 1. And when it actually—

PERSON 3. Who gets the credit? Sure. We don't all like one another. We don't all enjoy working together. Maybe we only did this because we absolutely had to.

PERSON 4. But we did it. We did it together. And it's done and it's over and—

PERSON 2. We won.

PERSON 3. We actually won this huge massive victory and whatever happens next it won't change the fact that we won. This story is over and we don't have to be in the same room ever again if we don't want to.

PERSON 4. We can do other things.

PERSON 5. Frankly I'm a bit tired of flash mobs.

A. I know I'll be fine. I know. I just . . . those triggers aren't going to disappear. Or if they're gone, they're floating inside, still.

T. We've done the work.

A. I'd just, I'd really like an anti-trigger. Something to hold on to, something that makes sense when the other things don't.

T. Something safe.

A. Something tangible. Something concrete.

(*A pause*)

And I know the law doesn't make sense most of the time, I said that, I meant it. It's useless or it's violent or it's just bad. But also, it's words that . . . sometimes it's words that I can hold on to. Words that can actually do something. Sometimes.

PERSON 4. I know what you mean. I was in court that day.

T. So hold on to that moment. Hold on to how you felt when they announced the verdict.

A. No, not that moment. I mean that was great. But that was also just these men and women in their fifties, sixties, sitting on a raised pedestal telling us they approved of our lives.

PERSON 4. I was thinking about the moment you were arguing our case in court. You and the others.

A. I felt someone was speaking up for me. I heard my voice in that room. And whatever happened, whatever the outcome, I was done apologizing.

PERSON 4. The decision was not going to change much, but at that moment, I felt less suffocated.

A. In that moment I didn't have to apologize for being who I was, for loving as fiercely as I do, for wanting everyone else to know.

PERSON 4. Maybe we will never agree on anything again.

A. But that day, it felt like nothing could stop us.

A long pause as the characters position themselves in a row along the length of the stage, alternating to face different sets of audience members. A and T will rise to join them at either end of this row.

PERSON 2. Your lordships, we stand before you today in the matter of *Navtej Singh Johar v. Union of India*.

A. At that moment, I was the ten-year-old again.

PERSON 1. This is a matter that affects the lives of millions of LGBTQ persons in the country.

A. But this time, someone was speaking up for me.

PERSON 3. We argue that Section 377 of the Indian Penal Code is unconstitutional.

A. This time, I had a voice.

PERSON 4. We have waited.

PERSON 5. We have waited a hundred and fifty-eight years.

PERSON 1. We have waited and watched as our fundamental freedoms have remained restrained under a colonial-era law, forcing us to live as second-class citizens.

PERSON 2. This case is about more than decriminalizing conduct which has been proscribed by a colonial law.

PERSON 3. This case is about an aspiration to realize the Constitution, to realize the worth of equal citizenship.

T. Our petitioners stand in this courtroom before you and ask you a question.

PERSON 4. How strongly must we love, knowing we are unconvicted felons?

PERSON 5. How long do we have to wait?

T. And so, your lordships . . .

PERSON 2. In the matter of *Navtej Singh Johar v. Union of India*—

PERSON 4. In the matter of *Anwesh Pokkuluri*—

PERSON 3. In the matter of *Naz Foundation*—

T. In the matter of *Voices Against 377*—

PERSON 1. In the matter of *Akkai Padmashali*—

PERSON 2. In the matter of millions of LGBTQ citizens in this country who have waited. In the matter of my clients who have lived their lives in the shadow of a law, waiting.

A. We stand before you, and tell you that we are done waiting.

EPILOGUE

The participants hold their formation for a few seconds, and abruptly break off. We are back in the space of the meeting, it has come to an end, and everybody proceeds in a business-like fashion to gather their belongings. A remains onstage, looking for something. He is joined by Person 3, who holds up a bag and clears his throat. At this point A has his back to Person 3.

PERSON 3. Hey. Hi. Mr Hufflepuff bag!

> (*As A turns around to face Person 3. We once again hear the opening bars of 'All You Need is Love'. Person 3 ignores this. A looks a bit stunned, then shakes his head, an action which is accompanied by the music going down.*)

> You left your bag?

A. Oh thanks.

PERSON 3. You didn't speak much at the meeting.

A. Oh, I've just been in a different headspace.

PERSON 3. Looked like you were talking to yourself.

A. Yeah that happens a lot.

PERSON 3. It was cute.

A. I think you meant to say terrifying.

PERSON 3. It shows you have personality.

A. Oh, I have lots of personalities.

PERSON 3. Ha! I'm Firoz.

A. I'm—I'm actually leaving.

PERSON 3. Diligent Hufflepuff off for the next meeting.

A. Yes, I have therapy.

PERSON 3. Saturday-evening therapy that's a fun weekend plan.

A. It's actually pretty entertaining. For my therapist anyway, I think.

PERSON 3. I always schedule mine on Thursday afternoons.

A. Ah you go—

PERSON 3. Three years this month.

A. That's—

PERSON 3. A lot of emotional work? Yeah, I'm super emotionally mature.

A. Great, I—

PERSON 3. I'm also emotionally available.

A. I'm sure your therapist is very proud.

A starts to walk away.

PERSON 3. So, I'm going to do a Gryffindor thing and ask if you'd like to get a drink.

A. Oh, that's really nice, I just . . . I'm . . . I'm doing this vacation thing—

PERSON 3. Oh, are you not from here?

A. No, like a vacation from dating.

PERSON 3. OK sure.

A. And also, you wouldn't want to—I'm a bit of a—I hear voices.

PERSON 3. What are these voices telling you?

A. Right now I can hear this Beatles song in my head.

PERSON 3. 'All You Need is Love'?

A. Wait, what, how did you—

PERSON 3. They're actually playing it downstairs. For the flash mob?

Pause as this registers.

A. Right. Anyway, it was nice meeting you, Firoz.

A starts to walk away.

PERSON 3. We don't have to call it a date.

A. Just two strangers getting a drink?

PERSON 3. We're not strangers. I know that you're a Hufflepuff and that you talk to yourself.

A. You and everyone who takes the Yellow Line.

PERSON 3. The alcohol's on me?

A. Generous.

PERSON 3. I'll even order the third cheapest wine on the menu?

A. Extravagant.

PERSON 3. I also make a really good cup of coffee the next morning?

A. How do you know there's going to be a next morning?

PERSON 3. I don't. I have no idea where this goes. Isn't that the fun part?

They stay frozen, looking at each other, as the closing bars of 'All You Need Is Love' get louder.

BIBLIOGRAPH-ISH NOTES

Love and Reparation is located in the space between the real and the fabulated. Here's a bit more on the real.

Contempt's trial scenes draw upon unofficial transcripts of the Supreme Court of India's hearings in 2012, available on the website of the Alternative Law Forum (altlawforum.org). I've also relied upon my recollections from these hearings as recorded in my essays:

'The Road to Decriminalization: Litigating India's Anti-Sodomy Law', *Yale Human Rights and Development Law Journal* 16(1) (2013). Available at: https://bit.ly/3vd0DsZ (last accessed on 20 April 2021).

'The Quality of Mercy, Strained: Compassion, Empathy, and Other Irrelevant Considerations in Koushal v. Naz', *NUJS Law Review* 6(4) (2013). Available at: https://bit.ly/3aA4MPT (last accessed on 20 April 2021).

Orinam (377.orinam.net) is an invaluable archive for materials related to the 377 litigation.

Pride relies less extensively on courtroom exchanges, but where it does, I've drawn upon the Alternative Law Forum's primer, *Right to Love* (2018; available at: https://bit.ly/3sJSpa7). Besides containing a shorter transcript of a much shorter set of hearings, this is a careful reading of key themes in the *Navtej Singh Johar v. Union of India* decision. It also contains a significantly more detailed timeline of the litigation than the one placed towards the start of this book. I've also relied on a series of dispatches I'd written from the courtroom, one of which is up on *National Herald* ('How Strongly Must We Love?', 12 July 2018) and the rest of which are available on the *Orinam* website.

A wealth of civil-society reports have informed litigation efforts across the decades. The stories painstakingly put together in these documents inform the narratives in both plays. The AIDS Bhedbhav Virodhi Andolan's *Less Than Gay. A Citizens' Report of the Status of Homosexuality in India* (New Delhi, 1991, available at: http://bit.ly/2GkwbGk) was one of the first reports of its kind, and continues to be an exemplar for the manner in which it weaves together personal narratives within a broader story of social justice. Other reports that I have relied upon directly or indirectly include: The India Centre for Human Rights and Law's *Humjinsi* (1999); The Karnataka chapter of the People's Union for Civil Liberties' *Human Rights Violations against the Transgender Community* (2003; available at: https://bit.ly/3nff5he); Human Rights Watch's *This Alien Legacy. The Origins of 'Sodomy' Laws in British Colonialism* (2008; available at: https://bit.ly/3ayCl4G); United Nations Development Programme–India's *Legal Recognition of Gender Identity of Transgender People* (2012; available at: https://bit.ly/-3aBpa30); LABIA's *Breaking the Binary* (2013; available at: https://bit.ly/-3vbUVYh); Ondede's *Report on the Human Rights Violations against Transgenders in Karnataka* (2013; available at: https://bit.ly/-3xlFvmb); the Coalition for Sex Workers and Sexuality Minority Rights' *Dignity First: One Year of Resistance to Re-criminalisation of LGBT Lives* (2014; available at; https://bit.ly/3etrQ3S); the

International Commission of Jurists' *Unnatural Offences: Obstacles to Justice in India Based on Sexual Orientation and Gender Identity* (2017; available at: https://bit.ly/3dJNEJv) and *Living with Dignity: Sexual Orientation and Gender Identity-Based Human Rights Violations in Housing, Work, and Public Spaces in India* (2019; available at: https://bit.ly/3vcuIsH).

I've also found a number of memoirs, anthologies and edited collections immensely valuable. Ashwini Sukthankar's *Facing the Mirror: Lesbian Writing in India* (New Delhi: Penguin Books, 1999) and Gautam Bhan and Arvind Narrain's *Because I Have a Voice: Queer Politics in India* (New Delhi: Yoda Press, 2005) are among the earliest anthologies of queer writing from the country. Alok Gupta and Arvind Narrain's *Law Like Love: Queer Perspectives on Law* (New Delhi: Yoda Press, 2011) and Minal Hajratwala's *Out! Stories from the New Queer India* (Mumbai: Queer Ink, 2013) provide accounts of the possibilities that emerged in the wake of the Delhi High Court's *Naz Foundation* verdict. A. Revathi's *The Truth about Me: A Hijra Life Story* (New Delhi: Penguin Books, 2011) and *A Life in Trans Activism* (New Delhi: Zubaan Books, 2016) and Parmesh Shahani's *Gay Bombay: Globalization, Love and (Be)longing in Contemporary India* (New Delhi: Sage, 2008) are important memoirs that also braid their personal accounts within broader political/theoretical narratives. Naisargi Dave's *Queer Activism in India: A Story in the Anthropology of Ethics* (New Haven, CT: Duke University Press, 2012) is a wonderfully narrated ethnography of early organizing efforts with a particular focus on lesbian communities.

The ancient night of revelry that opens *Contempt* comes from Plato's *Symposium*. I've used the translation by W. H. D Rouse (New

York: New American Library, 1984) read with Randall Baldwin Clark's 'Platonic Love in a Colorado Courtroom: Martha Nussbaum, John Finnis, and Plato's Laws in *Evans v. Romer*' (*Yale Journal of Law and the Humanities* 12[1] [2000]; available at: https://bit.ly/-3xgD6t9). Further informing my understanding—and experience—of eros are David Halperin's 'Platonic Eros and What Men Call Love' (*Ancient Philosophy* 5 [1985]: 161–204) and Anne Carson's *Eros the Bittersweet* (Princeton, NJ: Princeton University Press, 1986).

Finally, in thinking about repair and reparation—besides Melanie Klein's *Love, Guilt and Reparation* (New York: Vintage Classics, 1998), I found Julia Kristeva's *Melanie Klein* (New York: Columbia University Press, 2001) immensely helpful. Also significant in their unpacking of repair are Elizabeth V. Spelman's *Repair: The Impulse to Restore in a Fragile World* (Boston, MA: Beacon Press, 2002) and Eve Kosofsky Sedgwick's gorgeous essay 'Paranoid Reading and Reparative Reading, or, You're So Paranoid, You Probably Think This Essay Is about You' from her book *Touching Feeling: Affect, Pedagogy, Performativity* (New Haven, CT: Duke University Press, 2003, pp. 123–52).

ACKNOWLEDGEMENTS

The first draft of *Contempt* was written under the generous guidance of Neel Chaudhari as part of the Tadpole Repertory's Writer's Room Summer Workshop of 2016. From there, the 15-minute script grew through feedback and discussions with Rupali Samuel, Anirudh Nair, Bhamati Sivapalan, Daniel Elam, Akhil Katyal, Swar Thounaojam, Jake Oorloff, Sanhita Ambast and Ajita Banerjie. I am grateful to the Floating Space Theatre Company in Colombo for performing the first staged reading of this play in July 2017, and to the staff and students of the O. P. Jindal Global University for engaging with the production in its early stages. The version of *Contempt* that you see before you initially emerged in print under the careful editorial guidance of Oberon Books and Serena Grasso and I am very grateful to them, as well as to Tasmine Airey, William Gregory and the other members of the Arcola Queer Collective in London for their support and encouragement. Thanks also to the team at Oddbird Theatre in Delhi for their faith in the script at an early stage in the process.

Pride was conceptualized and workshopped scene by scene through conversations with a range of friends. In different ways, these individuals have helped me think through the ideas I was attempting to convey with patience and grace and I thank them: Rohini Sen, Andrew Halladay, Tejaswi Shetty, Meghal Mehta, Niha

Masih, Nafisa Ferdous, Q, Mihira Sood and Suhasini Sen. I'm also grateful for the careful feedback on the script from Lekha Sridhar, Mythili Vijay Kumar, Rohini Malur, and Deepa Dharmadhikari. I am grateful to Abhina Aher for her incandescent portrayal of Kokila for nine shows of *Contempt* and for generously lending fragments of her story for one of the accounts in *Pride,* to Arshiya Qasba Nabi and Kalyani Menon for their incredible backstage support every step of the way and to all the various individuals who have stepped in to read and perform these two scripts over the last two years.

I thank Sandip Roy and Bishan Samaddar of Seagull Books for their faith in the project and for the vision of putting the two plays together as a single volume. Tarun Khaitan generously penned the foreword to this text; Daniel Elam, Ann Genovese, Geeta Patel, Klaus Mueller and Rahul Rao offered their gracious and humbling endorsements.

As a reader, your first encounter with these works is mediated through the preface to this book. Writing those few pages was a journey in and of itself, informed by the generous conversations and community that I've found myself a part of in Melbourne. I'm particularly grateful to Peter Rush and Shaun McVeigh who are in the process of supervising my PhD, to Andre Dao, Johanna Commins, Toerien Van Vyk and Tim Lindgren for endless conversations that have refracted their way back into this work, and to Will Dawson for his kind, patient, practice of love. With Australia's COVID-informed border restrictions, this has been the longest period I have gone without seeing my parents and sister. Their support through this process has been unwavering and I thank them. My very talented sister Abir Sheikh threw a range of wonderful cover ideas at me, some of which found their way into the final design for this book.

To the lawyers and activists who have fought tirelessly across decades, who continue to fight battles that only seem to get more difficult, I dedicate this book. Thank you for your deeply inspiring practice of law and love.